1   ⌐anged
The World:

A Study in Science,
History and Culture

by Michael & Lynn Borich

Thank you to our good friend and inimitable graphic designer Phillip Secca for the cover.

www.PublishTheWord.com

ISBN-13: 978-1493781508

ISBN-10: 1493781502

Chapters

Charlemagne
Dante Alighieri
Nicolas Copernicus
Michelangelo
Sir Francis Bacon
William Shakespeare
Galileo Galilei
Johannes Kepler
Rene Descartes
Blaise Pascal
Robert Boyle
Sir Isaac Newton

George Frideric Handel
Johann Sebastian Bach
Franz Joseph Haydn
Wolfgang Amadeus Mozart
Napoleon Bonaparte
Ludwig Van Beethoven
Michael Faraday
Sojourner Truth
Gregor Mendel
Louis Pasteur
Lord Kelvin
Leo Tolstoy
Max Planck
George Washington Carver
Sun Yat-sen
Werner von Braun
Aleksandr Solzhenitsyn
Albert Einstein
Stephen Hawking
Cassie Bernall

. . .and 70 others

To our two sons,
Aeron Michael and Shawn Mark

How It Began

This book began as discussions with international students, especially English language students in the People's Republic of China during our two years teaching English at Qingdao University.

Our Chinese students had grown up with an atheistic worldview, a limited background in Western Culture and almost no understanding of Christian beliefs. They often were puzzled that religion was important to us. From a young age they had been warned against such "old superstitions."

In China's new, rapidly changing, materialistic society, the one "god" they might admit to worshipping is Education which promises true believers escape from the poverty and provinciality of old, feudalistic society. If some of their grandmothers still practiced Buddhist or Taoist rituals by celebrating Tomb Sweeping Day or burned paper money for departed relatives at the New Year, it was to honor tradition, but most of our students secretly disdained such ignorant thinking.

However, if their well-educated professors from America, England and Australia considered religion and faith in a God and a Holy Book and prayer as more than just cultural artifacts, students wanted to know why. Foreign "experts," as teachers like us were called are strictly forbidden to proselytize, but on occasions like Christmas such discussions, even in the classroom, are quite natural.

Just two blocks from our campus an official Chinese government church held a Friday night youth service, so we would occasionally go out of curiosity and take a student or two as translators. Inevitably, questions would arise, discussions ensue and the big questions of life, death and the afterlife provided opportunities to begin ongoing dialogues with students that even continued via email after we returned to the States.

Out of those give-and-take sessions the text for this book was born.

Many of our American students, sadly, have the same lack of basic knowledge about Christianity as our international students. So we hope this simple, reasoned approach to thinking about the big questions will also be a resource to any open-minded, truth-seeking student.

Other than Lynn's testimony, most of the material is direct research from a variety of sources. To make it more readable, we have chosen not to include the hundreds of source citations that we would require of our students, but anyone who wants a list can email us through our website:

www.Publishtheword.com

Preface

Why have civilizations throughout history arisen only to later collapse and fall:

Egypt under the Pharaohs, the ancient empires of Babylonia or Persia under Xerxes, then the Greeks of Alexander, the Romans of the Caesars, the Incas or Aztecs or the imperial dynasties of China? What forces created these powerful societies? Have superior armies or weapons been the reason why one culture conquers another?

The Germans coined a term long before Hitler's Third Reich plunged half the world into the most horrific war ever -- *weltgeist* or "world spirit," which means a global force greater than any one ruler or government, as if the inevitable changes that shape one society are so powerful as to affect entire continents or areas of the earth.

In his book which won the 1998 Pulitzer Prize, *Guns, Germs and Steel: the Fate of Human Societies,* author Jared Diamond poses the question why Eurasian culture as a whole survived and conquered others while cultural groups in Africa or South America even today remain far behind in technological progress, political or social organization. Diamond argues against genetic or racial differences. Nor does he believe one people group is by nature more intelligent or resourceful than others. Geography may be a factor, also agricultural development and immunity to germs and disease.

Any study of science, history and culture must be broad in scope, but deep in analytic thought to uncover the real reasons why one society seems to thrive, advance and dominate others, while another is defeated, enslaved or even exterminated.

Written history can be biased by who does the writing. Our bias is not to examine the socio-biological reasons why Rome declined or the Mongols ruled Asia in the 12th and 13th Centuries under Genghis and Kublai Khan.

We want to challenge readers to think more seriously about *the greatest force* that affects all life on earth and our human destiny -- the unseen power that moment by moment sustains the universe. The same life force that moves global weather patterns to create typhoons or tectonic plate shifts and earthquakes deep inside the earth also causes a human baby's heart the size of an apple seed to begin to beat.

We know how the heart muscle rhythmically contracts to pump blood throughout the body – six quarts on a daily 12,000 mile circuit of arteries and veins. The average heart beats 72 times a minute, over 100 thousand times a day, 42 million beats per year or almost 3 billion times in a person's life. It beats involuntarily, without our willing it. What force causes the first beat? More importantly, why? Why does our heart beat, even as we sleep? Who or what programmed our marvelous human bodies?

Who or what is the force behind all of life?

Common Sense Thinking -- In March of 1776 Thomas Paine, one of America's Founding Fathers, published his pamphlet *Common Sense.* He reasoned in plain language that the 13 Colonies should become independent of England and form a free, republican government to guarantee liberties for all citizens. His ideas made sense and motivated the colonists to take action. Several months later the new country was born.

We know ideas can be a force for change. But how do we *know* what we *know*? And do we *believe* what

9

we cannot know for certain? Do reason and logic end where belief and faith begin? Thinking people everywhere ask these questions.

The ancient Greeks – especially Socrates, Plato and Aristotle – wrestled with the same questions. What can we know for sure? Their principles for rational thinking, of how one idea leads to others, of how asking questions stimulates possible answers, of how we logically organize knowledge-- known as rhetoric – influenced how we formed our modern political and legal systems. Consider our courts, for example:

A person is charged with a crime. A trial is held. Eyewitnesses give testimony. Are they credible? Evidence is presented. Is it convincing? Experts offer their ideas. Are they trustworthy? Claims and counter-claims are given. The jury weighs all the evidence and testimony. Reasonable doubts are examined. Discussion may continue for hours or days. Finally a verdict is reached – by reason and logic.

We invite you to be a jury of one. Be open-minded. Consider the following ideas with common sense. Ask questions. Raise objections. You won't be the first. For thousands of years we have struggled to make sense of life, death and the greatest force -- God.

Perhaps we are hard-wired at birth to seek answers to such questions. That makes us different from the animals. Maybe we cannot know everything with 100 percent certainty, but we can – through logical thinking – arrive at our own common sense verdict. . . beyond reasonable doubts. Consider the first question:

Is belief in a Supernatural Force – God – reasonable?

1. Is Belief in a Supernatural Force – God -- Reasonable?

Atheists would say no. There is no evidence. From the Greek "a-theos" meaning no-God, an atheist has one big problem: he makes an absolute claim he cannot prove. He says there is absolutely no evidence for a supernatural entity – a God -- in the entire universe!

But his absolute claim of no God is made from his limited knowledge. He has never left planet Earth. Can he know **with certainty** that God doesn't exist in some distant part of our galaxy? How does he know? He doesn't. We can only make an absolute claim about what we do know – not what we don't. His reasons are unreasonable.

If we say there is absolutely no life in the universe except on planet earth, how do we know for sure if we have not visited every galaxy? To make such a claim with limited knowledge is faulty thinking known as a logical fallacy. We should reasonably say, we **don't know** if life exists beyond planet Earth.

An *agnostic* or skeptic admits **we don't know for sure** – the evidence is lacking. "A-Gnostic" comes from the Greek word for knowledge – hence, no-knowledge. There may be a God, but we don't have enough knowledge to arrive at that conclusion.

A reasonable person, using common sense, should say "Let's reason together. Let's examine the evidence." An agnostic is generally open-minded. That is a reasonable starting point.

Throughout world history every culture group seems to have had a belief in a god or gods – the Greeks and Romans believed in a pantheon of gods on Mount Olympus. Incas and Aztecs created rituals to honor their gods. In Southeast Asia Hinduism worships millions of gods. In Native Americans, South Sea Islanders,

11

African tribal groups – belief in a transcendent being or gods is universal: poly-theism or many gods; pan-theism or god in natural forces; mono-theism, one God.

Judaism. Islam. Buddhism. Taoism. Christianity. Billions of people worldwide believe in a transcendent being or force greater than ourselves.

Why this universal belief? In the wisdom book of Ecclesiastes, the writer says, "God has set eternity in the hearts of men."

We seem to have an instinct to seek after God embedded in us at birth. It is natural and normal to want to know.

Just as a young child begins to explore the physical world by his developing senses – tasting every object he can put into his mouth, staring for long minutes at his fingers, listening to each new sound – all to gain knowledge -- we too, as our intellect develops, have an inner drive to seek knowledge of God.

King David, the shepherd king of ancient Israel, told his son these words about 3000 years ago:

"And you, my son Solomon, acknowledge the God of your father and serve him with wholehearted devotion and with a willing mind, for the Lord searches every heart and understands every motive behind the thoughts. If you seek him, he will be found by you."

Reasonable Conclusion #1 – Humans have an innate desire to seek knowledge of God.

2. Upon what evidence is our belief based?

Let's talk about belief for a moment. What is belief? Are *belief* and *faith* the same?

Every time we drive down a road in our car and are approached by an oncoming car coming toward us at 60 miles an hour, we have a reasonable belief that the other driver will stay in his lane and pass us by. Why? Why don't we automatically think that we will have a head-on collision and die? Because we have **reason to believe** the other driver has passed a basic driving test, knows the rules of the road, has experience driving, sees us approaching – all common sense reasons not to be paranoid, even though a two-ton vehicle traveling at such a speed so close to us could easily be a lethal weapon.

Have you ever flown? The same principle applies. You don't know the pilot. You don't know his training or experience. You don't know if he is drunk or fatigued. And yet, we have enough *faith to believe* an enormous 180 ton airplane made of metal can fly us to our destination by a pilot we trust our lives with.

Every time you enter a restaurant you reasonably believe the cook won't poison you. We believe an elevator won't break loose and plummet twenty floors. We have faith that we will awaken every morning, that our heart will continue beating without us willing it to beat. We believe our lives will continue until we grow old or get sick and die or some unexpected accident befalls us. We live by faith.

From our daily life experience we gain *experiential knowledge*, though many of our decisions – to drive on a highway or fly in a plane—are made with implicit faith. We don't know for sure if a drunk driver will veer into our lane. We can't be sure our plane won't have an engine failure. We *believe* we will be okay based on reasonable evidence.

Webster's New Collegiate dictionary offers two slightly different definitions of **belief**:

1) *trust or confidence placed in some person or thing*, and 2) *conviction of the truth of some statement, being or phenomenon when based on examination of* ***evidence***.

The definition of **faith** is similar – *something that is believed with strong conviction*.

The Bible offers another definition of faith: *faith is the* ***evidence*** *of things not seen*.

Did you notice the word "evidence" appeared a couple times?

Back to our court of law – what is the evidence for belief or faith in God?

Using common sense, let's consider **evidence found in the natural world** which should lead us to reasonably conclude God does exist and He wants us to know He exists.

In his letter written to first century believers in Rome, Italy, Paul of Tarsus writes: *"Since the creation of the world God's invisible qualities – his eternal power and divine nature – have been clearly seen,* ***being understood from what has been made****, so that men are without excuse."*

David, the shepherd king of ancient Israel, wrote in 1000 B.C. *"The heavens declare the glory of God; the skies proclaim the work of his hands."*

Of course, both these quotes begin with the assumption that God exists as evidenced by his handiwork – all of creation. The Bible begins with these words, *"In the beginning God created the heavens and the earth."*

14

But a rule of logic states we cannot begin reasoning at our conclusion. We only get to the end if we start at the beginning. To reason *deductively* we say: there is a God – just look at everything He created. To reason *inductively*, we must say: look at all of creation –how did it come to be?

How did the heavens come to exist? What about the incredible bio-diversity of life on earth? We know our parents' sexual union made us, but who made our very first ancestral parents?

Consider the common choices – 1) some powerful being created everything for a reason or 2) no being created anything: the universe and everything in it, our planet and all life on it, you, us and everyone who ever lived – came into existence by chance, over billions of years – we evolved; matter always existed, and at some point in time, a big bang occurred in the universe, and as chunks of meteors and asteroids shot off into space and cooled, some chemical elements combined and sprang to life and began to reproduce and eventually increased in complexity. . . until. .

Let's examine two interesting topics for scientific evidence: our home planet earth, and then our human cellular makeup. Here's the question we will pose: if we find what reasonably seems to be **intelligent design in nature** – not random chance – but intricate patterns of design, would it be reasonable to assume there is a designer?

If we stand in front of a building and see it rise above us, does our common sense tell us it just grew spontaneously from the earth or that some skillful builder built it? When we look at a painting, can we conclude from the evidence of the paint, which to our eyes seems to have been applied in some meaningful pattern, that there was a painter? Such a conclusion would seem reasonable -- common sense.

Can Science provide any evidence for God?

The Earth is 93 million miles from the Sun—a distance that happens to be just right for life to exist. The Sun is a giant fireball that gives off more energy in a single second than mankind has produced since the world began. It converts 8 million tons of matter into energy every single second and has an interior temperature of more than 20 million degrees Celsius. The 93 million miles of empty space between Earth and the Sun help stop the deafening noise and destructive pressure waves given off by the Sun as it converts matter into energy.

The Sun also produces radiation, a form of light that can damage our eyes and cause skin cancer. We receive some protection from a special gas known as "ozone." A layer of ozone in the stratosphere (about 12 to 18 miles off the earth's surface) screens much of the radiation from hitting earth. In addition, the Sun constantly sends out an invisible solar wind composed of tiny particles. These particles approach the Earth from outer space at a very high speed and could be fatal to humans. Instead, most of these particles are reflected back into space because of Earth's magnetic buffer.

Earth has exactly the right surface temperature for life. The average temperature is 11.3°C or about 53° Fahrenheit. On our neighbor closest to the sun, Venus, temperatures are a scalding 480°C, and on Mars, our other near neighbor, we would have to endure days and nights 100 degrees colder than earth. And Mars' thin atmosphere is mostly poisonous nitrogen, unsuitable to sustain life.

The Earth is tilted on its axis exactly right -- 23.5°. If it sat up straight in its orbit around the Sun, there would be no seasons. The tropics would be hotter and deserts would cover more of the earth. If we were tilted 90°, Earth would be ravaged by frigid winters and boiling summers.

At 240,000 miles from Earth, the Moon controls the movement of ocean tides. This movement cleanses shorelines and helps the delicate ecosystem of plant and animal life. Currents are a crucial part of the oceans. Without currents, water in the oceans would stagnate, causing sea life to perish. Our human existence depends upon the Moon's tides, which help to balance nature's delicate food chain.

The oceans, which cover about 72% of the Earth's surface, provide a reservoir of moisture that constantly evaporates and condenses and eventually falls as rain. Because water holds its temperature longer, it provides a natural heating/air-conditioning system for land areas on the Earth. The Earth's annual average temperature (53°F) is closely maintained by the great reservoir of heat found within the ocean waters.

As humans, we breathe in oxygen and breathe out carbon dioxide. Plants, on the other hand, take in carbon dioxide and give off oxygen – so we depend on the plant world for our constant, fresh oxygen supply. Approximately 90% of that oxygen comes from tiny, microscopic plants within the Earth's oceans and seas.

Most scientists agree the universe and our earth did begin at some point in time. An article in *U.S. News & World Report* of March 31, 1997 said, "New scientific revelations about supernovas, black holes, quarks, and the big bang even suggest to some scientists that there is a 'grand design' in the universe."

Two American National Aeronautics and Space Administration (NASA) scientists who won the 2006

Nobel Prize in Physics – Lawrence Smoot and John Mather – were architects of a 1989 cosmic background exploration named COBE that measured feeble remnants of the oldest light in the universe. This light displayed a "blackbody" spectrum and indicated the planetary universe began at a uniform temperature before expanding – thus lending support to what is known as the Big Bang theory.

If our universe came into existence as the result of a "Big Bang" that accidentally caused everything we see around us – trees, flowers, birds, fish, animals, people, and according to the United Nations Environmental Program's *Global Biodiversity Assessment,* approximately **1.75 million unique species** – all theoretically from a single, one-celled ancestor -- what are the statistical chances that Earth is *exactly* the right distance from the Sun? *exactly* the right distance from the Moon? has *exactly* the right diameter? *exactly* the right tilt on its axis? *exactly* the right amount of water on its surface? *exactly* the right atmospheric pressure? *exactly* the right amount of oxygen?

Could all of these things be "exactly right"— by accident? Or coincidence?

What does reason and common sense tell us?

According to Dr. Hugh Ross, who holds a PhD in astronomy from the University of Toronto and was a research fellow at the California Institute for Technology, for the universe to have the attributes necessary for physical life on earth, the probability of 332 specific parameters, such as axis tilt of the earth, surface gravity, magnetic field, atmospheric temperature, oxygen, nitrogen and carbon dioxide ratios -- the mathematical chance is less than 1 in 10 to the 282 power – that is equal to one chance in a million trillion trillion trillion trillion trillion trillion trillion trillion trillion trillion trillion trillion trillion trillion trillion

trillion trillion trillion trillion trillion trillion trillion trillion.

In their book *The Privileged Planet* Guillermo Gonzalez and Jay W. Richards recall a moment that caught the world's attention:

"On Christmas Eve, 1968, the Apollo 8 astronauts—Frank Borman, James Lovell, and William Anders—became the first human beings to see the far side of the Moon. The moment was as historic as it was perilous: they had been wrested from Earth's gravity and hurled into space by the massive, barely tested Saturn V rocket. Although one of their primary tasks was to take pictures of the Moon in search of future landing sites—the first lunar landing would take place just seven months later—many associate their mission with a different photograph, commonly known as *Earthrise*.

"Emerging from the Moon's far side during their fourth orbit, the astronauts were suddenly transfixed by their vision of Earth, a delicate, gleaming swirl of blue and white, contrasting with the monochromatic, barren lunar horizon. Earth had never appeared so small to human eyes, yet was never more the center of attention.

"To mark the event's significance and its occurrence on Christmas Eve, the crew had decided, after much deliberation, to read the opening words of Genesis: "In the beginning, God created the heavens and the Earth . . . ." The reading, and the reverent silence that followed, went out over a live telecast to an estimated one billion viewers, the largest single audience in television history."

Three years later Astronaut James Irwin, who drove the first lunar rover on the moon's surface, said: "The Earth reminded us of a Christmas tree ornament hanging in the blackness of space. As we got farther and farther away it diminished in size. Finally it shrank to the size of a marble, the most beautiful marble you can imagine.

That beautiful, warm, living object looked so fragile, so delicate, that if you touched it with a finger it would crumble and fall apart. Seeing this has to change a man, has to make a man appreciate the creation of God and the love of God."

Harvard-educated astrophysicist John A. O'Keefe of NASA, said, "If the universe had not been made with the most exacting precision we could never have come into existence. It is my view that these circumstances indicate the universe *was created* for man to live in."

Humanity – did we evolve from a single cell of life that began. . . how?

Here's an idea: you are walking along a quiet beach. You can see where waves have washed up on the sand dunes and created an interesting ripple pattern. What do those symmetrical, repeated lines tell us? Can nature or forces of nature create a design? Yes. Is this evidence of a designer? Of course not.

But let's say we walk a little farther and come upon the shape of a heart carved into the sand enclosing the words *John loves Sally*. Would we conclude the natural motion of the waves created the heart and words? Of course not.

The specific design and the words suggest an intelligence at work – the heart and words are information. The sand ripples may have just happened from natural wave motion, but the heart and the words were created by someone for a purpose.

Consider DNA, the Instruction Manual for all life:

Deoxyribonucleic Acid. DNA, is found in our cells, the smallest living units in our bodies. Every living organism is made of cells. Microscopic organisms such as algae, bacteria, and protozoa are made of only one cell. A person, on the other hand, is made of trillions of specialized cells. Skin cells, brain cells, nerve, muscle and bone cells work together to form organs which make the systems of the body. Inside every cell is the **information** that determines what function the cell performs. DNA carries the unique genetic code of every person – eye color, hair texture, skin pigment, body type, facial features and so on. This DNA information in the chromosomes of each cell nucleus could be compared to biological software.

Microsoft founder Bill Gates is not a scientist, but he does know a little something about computer software. In his autobiography *The Road Ahead* he writes "DNA is like a computer program, but far, far more advanced than any software we've ever created."

Francis Crick, who received a Nobel Prize for discovering the structure of DNA said *in Life Itself*, "An honest man, armed with all the knowledge available to us now, could only state that, in some sense, the origin of life appears at the moment to be almost a miracle."

The big question is: did DNA develop during the evolutionary process – millions of years of time plus chance? How did that happen? Or was there a DNA software programmer, an intelligent being capable of embedding the complex genetic data in each and every cell in each and every living creature on earth? What is the statistical probability of the first cell writing its own self-replication instruction book?

Scientists have estimated the amount of information in a single DNA cell would equal all 30 volumes of the *Encyclopedia Britannica*, three or four times over – 100 volumes! And that is only one cell! Let's look at DNA a little closer.

The DNA coil, known as a double-helix, inside every one of our body's one hundred trillion cells contains a four-letter chemical alphabet – in endless configurations -- that spells out precise assembly instructions for all the proteins from which our bodies are made. Rick Gore, writing in *National Geographic* said, "Each cell is a world brimming with as many as two hundred trillion tiny groups of atoms called molecules. Our 46 human chromosome 'threads' linked together would measure more than six feet. Yet the cell nucleus that contains them is less than four ten-thousandths of an inch in diameter."

Dr. Stephen Meyer, who earned his Ph.D. from Cambridge University for a dissertation on the history of life-origin biology and the methodology of the historical sciences, demonstrated in his book *Evidence of Design in the Universe* that no hypothesis has come close to explaining how information got into biological matter by naturalistic means.

On the contrary, he said that whenever we find a sequential arrangement that is complex and corresponds to an independent pattern or function, this kind of information is always the product of intelligence. "Books, computer codes, symphonic scores, and DNA all have these properties," he said. "We know books, computer codes and scores are designed by intelligence, and the presence of this type of information in DNA also implies an intelligent source."

Can we explain DNA solely by physical-chemical laws? The base elements, sugars, and phosphates comprising the nucleotides in DNA are ordinary chemicals that do react according to ordinary laws. Yet those same laws do not explain how the chemicals came to function as a cellular software code.

We know natural physical forces do create either random patterns, like wind blowing leaves against a fence, or else ordered, repetitive structures, like ripples on a beach. But modern information theory teaches that neither random nor repetitive structures carry high levels of information. Nancy Pearcey, author of *The Soul of Science,* suggests DNA is too complex to just simply occur without a reasonable explanation:

The information content of any structure is defined as the minimum number of instructions needed to specify it. For example, a random pattern of letters has a low information content because it requires very few instructions: 1) Select an alphabet letter and write it down, and then, 2) Do it again, such as E-E-E-E-E.

A highly ordered, but repetitive pattern, likewise, has low information content. Wrapping paper with "Happy Birthday" printed all over in gold letters is highly ordered, but it can be created with very few instructions: 1) Write "H-a-p-p-y-B-i-r-t-h-d-a-y," and then, 2) Do it again.

By contrast, a structure like DNA with high information content requires a large number of instructions. If you want your computer to print out the "Declaration of Independence," you must specify every letter, one by one. There are no shortcuts.

This is the kind of order we find in DNA. It would be impossible to produce a simple set of instructions telling a biochemist how to synthesize the DNA of even the simplest bacterium. You would have to specify every chemical "letter," one by one.

Logically, could we pile individual letters of printer's type on a beach and expect that millions of years of wind and waves would rearrange the letters into the text of the "Declaration of Independence"? Could we reasonably conclude some intelligence arranged the letters into a meaningful pattern? If we visit Mount Rushmore in South Dakota would we assume that wind, rain and erosion created the faces of four American presidents?

Or would we conclude some intelligence created the faces?

Dr. Werner Arber, a Swiss Microbiologist who won the 1978 Nobel Prize for Medicine, said: "The most primitive cells may require at least several hundred different specific biological macro-molecules. How such already quite complex structures may have come together, remains a mystery to me. The possibility of the existence of a Creator, of God, represents to me a satisfactory solution to this problem."

Consider the geologic record

Geo/rock and *logic*/reason provide ancient evidence that modern technology is only now able to interpret. Dr. Stephen Meyer refers to the Cambrian period, during the early Paleozoic era, as an important point in the history of life on earth when most major groups of animals we know today first appear in the fossil record. Known by scientists as the "Cambrian Explosion," *in a relatively short time* a dazzling array of new life forms suddenly appeared, fully formed, in the rock strata -- with no prior transitions. At least 25 major animal phyla sprang into existence, each phylum exhibiting a unique architecture, blueprint or structural body plan.

Familiar examples of basic animal body plans are cnidarians (corals and jellyfish), mollusks (squids and shellfish), arthropods (crustaceans, insects, and trilobites), echinoderms (sea star and sea urchins), and the chordates, the phylum to which all vertebrates belong, including human beings.

This would have required the infusion of massive amounts of new biological information – DNA. As organisms become more complex, they must become larger and assume more sophisticated body types, with hard skeletons, for example, so they can acquire the different features they need to survive. Complex development requires complex DNA.

How did complex DNA occur without sufficient time for a natural, evolutionary process?

Dr. Meyer and co-authors, P.A. Nelson and Paul Chien, in "Biology's Big Bang," conclude, "The major body plans that arise in the Cambrian period exhibit considerable disparity from one another. Though all Cambrian and subsequent animals fall clearly within one of a limited number of basic body plans, each of these body plans exhibit clear morphological differences. The animal body plans (as represented in the fossil record) **do not grade imperceptibly one into another**, either at a given time or over the course of geological history."

Instead, the body plans of the animals characterizing the separate phyla maintain their differences from all the other types of animals – as if at a creative intelligence all at once infused each species, *after its own kind,* with new DNA information.

Naturalist and father of evolutionary theory, Charles Darwin himself said in *The Origin of Species* (1859): "Why then is not every geological formation full of such intermediate links? Geology assuredly does not reveal any finely graduated organic change, and this is the most obvious and serious objection that can be urged against the theory."

"Information is the hallmark of mind," said Dr. Meyer. "And purely from the evidence of genetics and biology, we can infer the existence of a mind that's far greater than our own -- a conscious, purposeful, rational, intelligent designer who's amazingly creative."

Look at another example: the human eye

Did you know that the human eye has 40 million nerve endings, the focusing muscles move an estimated

100,000 times a day, and the retina contains 137 million light sensitive cells? A single eye is an engineering marvel. Even today the most advanced scientific technology cannot create a fully functioning human eye that could be transplanted into blind people.

Dr George Marshall, an eye-disease researcher from the University of Glasgow, Scotland said, "Most people see the miracle of sight. I see a miracle of complexity on viewing things at 100,000 times magnification. The retina is probably the most complicated tissue in the whole body. Millions of nerve cells interconnect in a fantastic number of ways to form a miniature 'brain.' Much of what the photoreceptors 'see' is interpreted and processed by the retina long before it enters the brain. The more I study the human eye, the harder it is to believe that it evolved."

Darwin said 150 years ago, "To suppose that the eye could have been formed by natural election, seems I freely confess, absurd in the highest degree."

In *The Origin of Species* Darwin stated: "If it could be demonstrated that any complex organ existed which could not possibly have been formed by numerous, successive, slight modifications, my theory would absolutely break down."

In other words, if science cannot prove the eye evolved step-by-step from simple, light-sensitive cells to the incredibly complex organ it is today, then how do we explain our ability to see? One way to think about this problem is what Lehigh University biochemist Dr. Michael Behe calls "irreducible complexity."

The eye is complex. Light passes through the cornea, the aqueous humor, pupil, iris, lens, vitreous body and several layers of the retina, stimulating nerve cells via ganglion fibers to transmit impulses to the brain. Vision occurs nearly instantaneously as a biochemical process at the molecular level – a transfer of light energy into information our brain interprets.

Behe says a system which meets Darwin's criterion is one which exhibits irreducible complexity: a single system composed of several interacting parts that contribute to the basic function. The removal of any one of the parts causes the system to cease functioning. You cannot reduce or take away any part of the eye – cornea, iris, lens or retina and still see. The complexity cannot be reduced.

Such a system cannot be produced gradually by slight, successive modifications of a precursor system. Any precursor to an irreducibly complex system is by definition nonfunctional.

Since natural selection requires a function to select, an irreducibly complex biological system would have to arise as a complete and fully integrated unit for natural selection to have anything to act on. All parts of the eye must be present.

It is almost universally conceded that such a sudden event would be irreconcilable with the gradualism Darwin envisioned.

Consider the humble mousetrap that consists of several parts. There is

(1) a flat wooden platform to act as a base;

(2) a metal hammer, which does the actual job of crushing the little mouse;

(3) a wire spring with extended ends to press against the platform and the hammer when the trap is set;

(4) a sensitive catch which releases when slight pressure is applied; and

(5) a metal bar which holds the hammer back when the trap is set and connects to the catch. Staples and screws hold the system together.

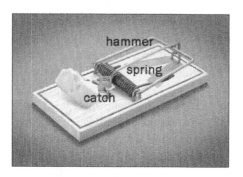

If any of the parts is missing the trap does not function.

If any one of the components of the mousetrap (the base, hammer, spring, catch, or holding bar) is removed, then the trap does not function. In other words, the simple little mousetrap has no ability to trap a mouse until several separate parts are all assembled.

Because the mousetrap is necessarily composed of several essential parts, it is irreducibly complex.

In addition to the eye, Behe says, other examples of irreducible complexity abound, including cilium, aspects of protein transport, blood clotting, closed circular DNA, electron transport, the bacterial flagellum, telomeres, photosynthesis, transcription regulation, and much more.

The natural world is full of examples which raise difficult questions – like irreducible complexity -- that have no simple, logical, naturalistic answers.

1971 Nobel Prize winner, Dr. Dennis Gabor, the Hungarian physicist who invented holography said, "I just cannot believe that everything developed by random mutations."

"For you created my inmost being; you knit me together in my mother's womb. I praise you because I am fearfully and wonderfully made." Psalm 139:13

Reasonable conclusion #2 – the design of the natural, observable world does point to an intelligent, master Designer.

3. Is The Bible A Supernatural Book?

If we can see design and order throughout creation from the atom to the far reaches of the universe, can we human beings – as the pinnacle of creation – assume we are also made with purpose and design? If we were made by a God and *in his image*, as some religions believe, would he hide Himself from us? Would He remain an invisible mystery or would He desire to communicate with us?

Three of the great, monotheistic world religions – Judaism, Christianity and Islam – believe God has communicated with mankind personally, as recorded in the sacred scriptures. The written record of the Bible gives us an account of God interacting with people from creation to future eternity.

How valid is God's revelation of Himself if the ancient texts were written by human beings? Is not the Bible, as it has so often been accused, a collection of myths, fables and invented tales that have changed over time? Has God really spoken to us? Has He visited planet earth? Have people seen Him?

Let's examine the evidence.

If creation leads us to see the handiwork of a Creator, what do the historical documents of the great religions tell us about the nature and character of God? The traditional Westminster (England) Catechism says, "The one and only true God is a *spirit*, or non-material being who is infinite, eternal and unchangeable."

Other primary texts, such as the Jewish Torah and Christian Bible describe Him as *omniscient*, knowing all things; *omnipresent*, present everywhere at the same time; *omnipotent*, able to do all things in harmony with His nature. He is holy, loving, merciful, gracious and benevolent. He is transcendent or existing in a realm above and outside His creation.

How do we know all this? Because He has told us directly, in personal, real-time encounters with a variety of human beings who recorded their experiences. Are these people trustworthy eyewitnesses?

The Bible (*biblia*, Latin for books) is literally a collection of 66 books, each unique, but with a distinct thematic unity, written by **40 *different authors*** over a period of 1500 years on three continents – Asia, Africa and Europe. The books are written in a variety of styles and genres: history, law, poetry, prophecy, wisdom literature, narrative, letters – but all with a common thread: God's relationship with His creation. It has been described as a supernatural book, unlike any other.

The Bible is the first book ever printed, the first book taken into space and to the moon by astronauts, the most read, most influential and best-selling book of all time, published in whole or in part in over 2,000 of the world's languages. According to the United Bible Societies over **5 *billion*** copies have been sold since 1815. No other book in the world comes close to the number of copies sold each year. What makes it different from other books?

God reveals Himself in it.

In the very second chapter of Genesis God makes Adam and Eve, our ancestral parents, stewards of His garden. He *talks* with them. We don't know in what form he appeared to them – if as a human or some other presence—but He *spoke* with them. They had a relationship. He provided food and every good thing they needed for life.

Later God *told* Noah to build an ark to prepare for a catastrophic flood. Noah heard and obeyed. God had *conversations* with Abraham and they entered into a covenant or sacred agreement together. God *appeared* to Moses in a burning bush and gave him specific instructions to lead his people from slavery to freedom. God led two million people through the desert and they *saw* his visible manifestation as a pillar of fire at night and a cloud by day. He *wrote* his law on tablets of stone all the people could see. He provided them daily with food and water.

On one occasion Moses asked to see God as He really is, but God replied that no human being could see God in His total essence and still live – the perfect, radiant glory of a pure and infinite God would be too overwhelming for a finite, imperfect being. (Exodus 3:20)

These examples are just from the first two books. Over 3,000 times in the Bible we read the words, "God said," or "God spoke." For those willing to study the ancient texts with an open mind, one fact becomes apparent:

Over time and in geographically and historically real places God did interact with people.

The texts become trustworthy if the authors are credible. Who were the authors? Where and when did they live? How can we verify the evidence of their lives and reasonably accept what they wrote as accurate and reliable?

The first five books of the Bible were written in Hebrew by Moses approximately 1400 B.C. – 3400 years ago. The events begin in Mesopotamia, also known as the Fertile Crescent where the three great continents meet.

After the creation account and mankind's fall from innocence into sin, we begin to find references to animal husbandry and farming, to communities of shared ethnicity and loosely-organized society. Moses documents peoples and events and places that can be cross-checked with other, non-biblical accounts and surviving historical artifacts. Science and archeology confirm what the Bible records.

The great flood, as detailed in Genesis 6, can also be found in the 11th tablet of the famous Babylonian *Gilgamesh* epic; king lists from ancient Sumer resemble the genealogy of Genesis 5; clay tables found recently in northern Syria parallel Genesis' descriptions of the commercial-legal-cultural-political life of civilizations during the 3rd century B.C. Numerous ancient texts in many languages confirm what the Bible records. Over 25,000 sites in biblical lands have been excavated which prove historical details of what Moses and others wrote.

Why would Moses be a reliable historian? He was adopted by the Egyptian king's daughter and raised in the court of Pharaoh. He learned to read and write Egyptian and received the equivalent of a university education. He also spoke and wrote Hebrew, his mother's native tongue. The text says Moses was "learned in all the wisdom of the Egyptians."

Scholars agree that Hebrew is one of the oldest and first phonetic languages. When Moses lived, most of the languages like Chaldean and Egyptian were pictorial based. Genesis was one of the first books written using an alphabet (24 letters). He recorded the development of early civilizations, the Exodus from Egypt, a census of the 12 tribes of Israel and laws God gave to the people. Moses lived 400 years before the Greeks destroyed Troy, 400 years before the first Hindu religious texts (Vedas) were written. He lived 1000 years before Buddha, Confucius, Lao-tzu, Plato or Aristotle.

The first texts were written on a variety of materials: papyrus, made from a reedy plant that grew in shallow water which was pressed, dried and polished smooth for writing; parchment, made from animal skins; dried clay tablets; wax tablets; pottery and inscribed stone. Most of the original documents, known as **autographs**, have not survived the centuries, except for fragments. But we do have copies and copies of copies that historians and archaeologists consider accurate and reliable.

Other Bible writers were equally well educated. Daniel was a prime minister to the kings of Babylon and Persia. Solomon was a king. Paul, who wrote 1/3 of the New Testament was a Roman citizen and highly-educated scholar who spoke at least 3 languages. Luke was a Greek physician with a mind of scientific inquiry who affirms at the beginning of his book that he "*carefully investigated everything from the beginning*," that he interviewed "*eyewitnesses*," and that he intended to "*write an orderly account*."

The first letter of John, a close companion to Jesus, records "what we have *heard*, what we have *seen* with our eyes, what we have *looked at* and our hands have *touched*" – in other words, eyewitness testimony and evidence. And Peter, another who traveled and lived with Jesus for three years wrote, "*we were eyewitnesses of his majesty*" (2 Peter 1:16). Again, we might ask the question: are they reliable witnesses and can we trust what they write? For centuries scholars have concluded yes.

What makes the Bible unique as a book is that God Himself inspires, guides and preserves the text.

To *inspire* literally means to "breathe into." *Expire* means to "breathe out," as when breath leaves the lungs, or *to die*, as when the soul leaves the body. Greeks believed

34

any of nine female goddesses called muses inspired them to write.

The Bible writers did not take direct dictation from God; they were not simply writing machines. Each writer's personal style is evident: Moses was factual and documentary; David was personal and poetic; Isaiah was literary; Jeremiah was passionate; Luke was detailed in real time and place, and Paul was intellectual and rhetorical. But God inspired all they wrote.

Paul writes to his adopted son, Timothy, "*All Scripture is given by **inspiration** of God*" or as another English translation reads, "*All Scripture is God-breathed,*" (2 Tim 3:16)

Peter tells us, "*Men spoke from God as they were moved by the Holy Spirit.*" (2 Peter 1:21).

What we find throughout the scriptures is evidence of God speaking to men, either in direct conversation, or indirectly by guiding their thoughts while writing.

"*Moses **wrote** all the words of the Lord.*" (Exodus 24:4)

Joshua, "**wrote** these words in the Book of the Law of God" (Joshua 24:26)

God told Isaiah, "*Take for yourself a large tablet and **write** on it*" (Isaiah 8:1)

John was commanded "***write**, therefore, what you have seen*" (Revelation 1:19)

The writer of Hebrews says, "*God, who at various times and in various ways **spoke** in time past to the fathers by the prophets, has in these last days spoken to us by His Son.*" (Hebrews 1:1).

Scholars of antiquity have analyzed the 39 Old and 27 New Testament books for over three thousand years to make certain of their authenticity. Universal consensus of historians, archaeologists, of literary textual critics, linguists, even scientists who have used new technologies to date the materials the texts are written upon all conclude that the places, people and events were recorded with an amazingly high degree of accuracy.

The overwhelming number of existing manuscripts increases the reliability of the texts. The earliest New Testament books – documentary narratives of Jesus' life written by his companions (Gospels), letters written by his followers, Luke's history (Acts) beginning with Jesus' return to heaven and the growth of the early church -- were all written between 50 and 95 A.D. That would be as soon as fifteen years after Jesus died until the persecution of the emperor Domitian at the end of the first century.

Copies of these original manuscripts were made almost immediately and widely circulated because Gutenberg's printing press was still 1400 years in the future.

Today we have more than 5,300 hand-copied Greek manuscripts of the New Testament. We have an additional 10,000 Latin copies, and another 9,300 written in Ethiopic, Armenian, Syriac, Arabic and various languages. In other words, nearly *25,000 ancient copies* of just the New Testament exist.

A crucial question is how old are the copies? Do they date to the time of the original autographs? If not, what is the time gap between the originals and the copies?

Beginning in 1898, two British archaeologists, Bernard Grenfell and Arthur Hunt, discovered thousands of papyrus fragments in the ancient garbage dump of Oxyrhynchus, Egypt. This site yielded public and private documents: codes, edicts, registers, official correspondence, census-returns, tax-assessments, petitions, court-records, sales, leases, wills, bills, accounts, inventories, horoscopes, private letters, classical literary works, as well as more than thirty-five manuscripts containing portions of the New Testament.

Some of the more noteworthy biblical papyrus manuscripts date to 100 years after their original composition. The collection is housed at Oxford University.

The Sir Arthur Chester Beatty Museum collection of artifacts and ancient manuscripts is housed in Dublin, Ireland. Papyrus #45 contains the four Gospels and much of the book of Acts. It dates to about 300 A.D. Papyrus #46 contains 10 letters penned by Paul and the book of Hebrews. Scholars say it was written about 200 A.D.

For about sixty years now a tiny papyrus fragment of the Gospel of John, the John Rylands papyri, has been the oldest "manuscript" of the New Testament. This manuscript (P52) has generally been dated to A.D. 125. To have a gap of 100 to 200 years may seem like a long time -- more than enough time for the original manuscripts to have become corrupted by errors or mistakes, some would say.

By comparison, today we have 643 existing copies of the most honored Greek classic, the *Iliad*, which Homer composed about 800 B.C. – the Biblical time of King Solomon. The oldest preserved copy of the *Iliad* dates from the 4th century B.C. -- *a gap of 400 years.*

For the philosophers Plato and Aristotle, we have 7 and 49 copies of their work that date from 900 A.D. and 1100 A.D. – *more than 1200 years* from when they were written.

We have 8 copies of the histories Herodotus wrote in 450 B.C., but only from 900 A.D. – a gap of 1400 years. We have 10 copies of Caesar's *Gallic Wars* written between 58-50 B.C., but 900 years after Caesar's day.

Sophocles plays – of which we have 193 copies – were written in the middle of the 4th century B.C. – during the golden age of Greece. But the oldest surviving copy comes from 1100 A.D., a time gap of 1400 years.

Great care was taken to copy and preserve the New Testament documents. *Over 25,000 copies, some less than 100 years* from the date the original autographs were composed, provide significant evidence to their reliability.

The most compelling evidence for transmission accuracy of Bible documents, however, comes from the Dead Sea Scrolls, found in eleven caves eight miles south of Jericho in 1947 by a Bedouin shepherd boy searching for a lost goat. He threw a stone into a cliff hole and heard pottery shatter. Within were several large jars containing leather scrolls wrapped in linen cloth. Because the jars had been sealed to keep out moisture and because of the extreme dryness of the desert climate, the scrolls had been well-preserved. . . **for 2000 years!**

Prior to finding the Dead Sea Scrolls, the earliest surviving Old Testament manuscripts came from the 10th century A.D. Now, according to Professor Timothy H. Lim, an editor on the international team producing principal editions of the texts for Oxford University Press, *25,000 inscribed fragments* from a millennium earlier – from the time of Jesus, himself – provide irrefutable evidence the sacred texts were copied with painstaking care and precision over the centuries. The number of different compositions represented on papyrus and parchment is almost one thousand, and they are written in three different languages: Hebrew, Aramaic, and Greek.

Thirty-nine manuscripts of the Psalms have been reconstructed from fragments left by the Essenes, a monastic farming community in what is today known as Khirbet Qumran. The scrolls, some of which have been carbon dated to the 1st century B.C., contain significant portions of every Old Testament book except Esther. The scroll known as the Great Isaiah Scroll, 24 feet long and 10 inches high, provided a complete Hebrew manuscript text of Isaiah --1000 years older than any previous manuscript. How exact was it?

Compared to the then oldest extant Massoretic text of Isaiah from 916 A.D., *95 percent* of the Dead Sea Scroll is word-for-word. The five percent difference is only in spelling variation or obvious slips of the pen. Antiquities Professor Millar Burrows said, "It is a matter of wonder that through a thousand years the text underwent so little alteration."

Ancient manuscripts are analyzed like fossils by paleographers and codicologists -- a type of manuscript archaeologist. Assessing document materials and inks, handwriting analysis, comparison with other manuscripts, where documents are found – all are carefully studied for clues that aid in authenticating texts.

Dating organic materials like papyrus and skins by estimating the half-lives of the degrading radiocarbon isotope has become a standard procedure of textual research, but a newer method known as Accelerator Mass Spectrometry is an even more precise dating method.

Gregory Bearman, a scientist at the Jet Propulsion Lab in Pasadena, developed multi-spectral imaging to decipher badly deteriorated script invisible to the human eye, and computer enhancing technology has been used at Princeton University as part of their Dead Sea Scrolls Project.

In 1993, an astonishing discovery was made at a tomb in Hubei province in east central China. Written on bamboo strips that have miraculously survived intact since 300 B.C., the "Guodian Laozi," is by far the earliest version of the ancient religious classic, *Tao Te*

Ching ever unearthed. Thought to be primarily the work of Lao-tzu, father of Taoism, who lived circa 604-531 B.C., Asian scholars proclaimed the discovery a decisive breakthrough in the understanding of this famous text: it provides the most conclusive *evidence* to date that the text was the work of multiple authors and editors over hundreds of years, rather than the achievement of a single individual writing during the Spring and Autumn period of the Eastern Zhou Dynasty. The newly discovered manuscript also establishes a time gap of only 250 years from when Lao-tzu actually lived.

We must apply the same standards in determining evidence, historicity and manuscript research methods to all literature of antiquity. If we conclude Chinese or Egyptian manuscripts to be valid, then using the same criteria, we must accept ancient Hebrew and Greek texts as being equally trustworthy.

Reasonable Conclusion #3 – 3500 years of evidence from archaeology, history and textual analysis provide reasonable proof that the Bible is a unique book, unlike any other. Over two billion people today in every culture and country in the world believe it is God's communication with humanity.

4. Was Jesus Just An Ordinary Man?

The Bible is more than a book about people and places: it is a book about a person – one like none other who ever lived.

Question: Why is Jesus Christ the center of human history? When the entire world celebrated the new millennium on January 1, 2000, from what date did we measure two thousand years? Beginning at what point in history do we record time prior to 2000 years?

The short answer is the date when Jesus Christ was born – January 1, A.D. 1 or "*anno domini*," the *year* of our *lord*. B.C. represents "before Christ." Though other calendars exist, notably Jewish, Muslim and Chinese – most people follow the Christian Era calendar begun by Dionysius Exiguus in A.D. 532 and later modified by Pope Gregory XIII. Why? Who was Jesus Christ that we should view time as what happened before and after his birth? Why is his impact upon the world so great?

James A. Francis, in a widely reprinted short essay from 1926 has written:

"Here is a man who was born in an obscure village, the child of a peasant woman. He grew up in another obscure village. He worked in a carpenter shop until He was thirty, and then for three years He was a traveling teacher. He never wrote a book. He never held an office.

He never owned a home. He never set foot inside a big city. He never traveled more than two hundred miles from the place where He was born. He had no credentials but Himself.

While still a young man, the tide of popular opinion turned against Him. His friends ran away. One of them betrayed Him. He was turned over to His enemies. He went through the mockery of a trial. He was nailed upon a cross between two thieves.

41

His executioners gambled for the only piece of property He had on earth while He was dying -- and that was His coat. When He was dead, He was taken down and laid in a borrowed grave through the pity of a friend.

Twenty centuries have come and gone and today He is the centerpiece of the human race and the leader of progress. I am far within the mark when I say that all the armies that ever marched, and all the navies that were ever built, and all the parliaments that ever sat, and all the kings that ever reigned -- put together -- have not affected the life of mankind upon this earth as powerfully as that One Solitary Life."

Let's examine the evidence of the man, the miracles and his message.

The name *Jesus* is a variation of Joshua or Yeshua, which means *The Lord saves*. To paraphrase what John, the gospel writer and beloved companion of Jesus said, "*God himself became a human being and lived among us*" (John 1:14). What a staggering claim to make! God became a human. Why?

The Greek and Roman gods were human-like and would leave Mount Olympus to interact with people, though we have no documentary evidence any of them ever existed except in mythology. Nor do we call this year, the year of our lord in reference to Zeus.

From the pantheon of 300 million Hindu gods, we have no historical data that Krishna or Vishnu ever entered our time-space world. But we can establish through the accuracy of Biblical texts that a historical Jesus Christ did exist. Even non-Christian authors have recorded his factual reality -- that he did live from about 1 to 33 A.D.

Tacitus, a respected Roman historian, wrote about *Christus*, who suffered death during the reign of Tiberius

Caesar at the hands of Pontius Pilate in Judaea. Other historical references to Jesus Christ occur in Flavius Josephus' *Antiquities*; and the writers Clement of Rome; Papias of Hierapolis in Asia Minor; Justin, a Greek philosopher born in Neapolis; Polycarp and Irenaeus, both of Smyrna and the historian Thallus, as cited in the writings of Julius Africanus.

Pliny the Younger (62-115 A.D.), a Roman governor of Turkey wrote in a letter to the Emperor Trajan about Christians brought before him: "They meet before daybreak. They sing hymns antiphonally and they worship Christ as if he were a god." And then he says, "They take an oath, but not an oath to do anything bad, rather an oath only to be good. Not to defraud people. Not to do anything evil."

We have no doubt Jesus lived.

How can we determine he was God in human flesh? Why did He become human?

We know from the beginning of the Jewish Torah/ Christian Old Testament that Adam and Eve's rebellion – their sin – separated them from God. Every descendent of our original parents enters life infected with the same spiritual-genetic disease – sin. We are like HIV infected babies born in Africa. This disease will eventually destroy the quality of our lives and bring death. But God's promise to Adam and Eve and throughout the Old Testament was that He would send a Messiah, a Savior for the whole world. No imperfect human, though, could reconcile humanity to a perfect God. Only God in human form, born of a woman, but without the birth defect of sin and who lived a perfect life could restore our right relationship with Himself. His promise of a Savior was repeated numerous times. **Prophecy** about the Savior adds credibility to God's promises.

Only God knows the future. He dwells outside our time-space universe which He sustains by His power, but as the Creator of time, He knows everything that will happen. If someone who lived 700 years ago – before Columbus came to America or during Kublai Khan's reign in the Yuan Dynasty – were to predict: 1) the city where you would be born, 2) that a messenger would herald your birth, 3) that you would enter the capital city riding on a donkey, 4) that your hands and feet would be pierced by spikes, 5) that you would be betrayed by a friend for 30 silver pieces, 6) that those 30 silver pieces would be used to buy a potter's field, 7) that you would stand silent before accusers, 8) that you would die nailed to a cross between thieves . . . what would be the statistical probability of all these predictions made 700 years before you were born coming true?

Professor Peter Stoner in his book *Science Speaks* calculated the chance that those eight prophecies coming true in any one person would be 1 in 10-to-the-17th power, that is 1 in 100,000,000,000,000,000.

To illustrate the chance of this occurring, cover the entire continent of Australia with silver coins – to a depth of two inches. Then mark one coin – only one – and drop it from an airplane anywhere over Australia. Now, blindfold a man and tell him to travel as far as he wants in any direction, but he can only pick up the silver coin you have marked. What chance would he have of choosing the right one? The same chance of eight specific prophecies coming true of one man who would live 700 years later -- the man is Jesus Christ.

God spoke through the prophets to confirm that Jesus Christ would be unlike any other human who ever lived. Not only did those eight prophecies come true about Jesus. ***Over 300 prophecies came true!*** What are the mathematical odds of this happening?

Jesus was more than unique, more than a man – He was God.

He said he was and he proved it by his life. In John's gospel (8:58), Jesus quoted the Old Testament book of Exodus (3:14) and said, of himself, "*Before Abraham was born, I Am*." This is the same phrase God used when Moses asked God's name. Those who heard Jesus speak these words were outraged because they understood he was calling himself God.

"I Am," is an unusual name. The complete phrase in Exodus is "*I Am Who I Am*," – thus clearly conveying in the ancient Hebrew language the present, continuing tense of the verb "to be": I Am eternally self-existent; I exist outside time; I was never born, nor will I die. *Yahweh* is this word for God's name in the original language, used over 5,000 times in the Old Testament, but considered too sacred to pronounce aloud. Jesus leaves no doubt that He and the Father are the same timeless, One, True, Living God (John 10:30).

Jesus also said in John's gospel of himself, "*I am the bread of life*," "*the light of the world*," "*the sheep gate*," "*the good shepherd*," "*the resurrection and the life*," "*the way, the truth and the life*," and "*the true vine*." He clearly knew who he was – that he had come down from above to save the world from sin and death. Why did other people not recognize who he was? Some did. His followers did and still do today.

The Miracles – was any other man ever like Jesus?

"*Believe me when I say that I am in the Father and the Father is in me, or at least believe on the **evidence of the miracles**.*" (John 14:11).

People throughout history have made outrageous claims; Jesus is not the only one who claimed to be God, but the **evidence** records he had a supernatural power. How do we explain the works he did? Yes, he did live among people we might consider superstitious, who

45

believed in angels and demons and miraculous powers, and no, we have no way to duplicate or verify with scientific certainty the miracles. But they are cross-referenced throughout the New Testament books. Luke, the Greek physician, investigated them thoroughly and sought eyewitness testimony before he included them in his gospel.

A 2003 Harris poll found that 84 percent of American adults think miracles can occur; 93 percent of Christians believe in miracles. Another study by the Institute for Religious and Social Studies in New York City asked physicians who were Christian, Jewish, Muslim, Hindu and Buddhist about miracles. Three out of four doctors surveyed believe that miracles -- unexplainable by medical science -- could occur. What were the acts of supernatural power that supported Jesus' claims to be God?

His Power Over Natural Forces:

*He turned over 100 gallons of water into wine.
*He calmed a violent storm.
*He walked atop the sea's surface.
*He fed 5,000 people with only two fish and
          five loaves of bread.
*He caused a fig tree to wither at his command.
*He healed numerous people of disease,
          blindness and paralysis.
*He set people free from demonic bondage.
*He raised from death a widow's son, a ruler's
          daughter and his friend Lazarus.
*He himself rose to life after being dead and
          entombed for three days.

We have eleven recorded instances of Jesus appearing to his followers after his resurrection, once to over 500 eyewitnesses. No miracle is more important than Jesus overcoming death and returning to life because now all humans everywhere have that same hope – that we might pass from death to life and escape the fear of what awaits us.

At least 35 miracles record the power of Jesus to overcome the laws of our natural world.

What other person in human history did what Jesus did? What other religious figure – Buddha, Lao-tzu, Mohammed – came back from death, is alive at this very moment at his Father's right hand in heaven and will return, as he promised, to establish His eternal kingdom? If miracles are not convincing evidence, examine the message of Jesus.

The Message of Jesus – Is Salvation to be found in anyone else?

Many will admit by pointing to the Sermon on the Mount or the golden rule of "do unto others as you would have them do unto you," that Jesus was a great moral teacher. But they stop short of saying what Jesus said of himself – that he was God in human flesh.

Confucius taught ethical principles – how one should relate to others in family, community and society. Buddha taught one could attain enlightenment, hence, non-existence by his noble eightfold path of right views and works. Mohammed required his followers to fulfill the five pillars of Islam, which include required prayers, giving to the poor, fasting and a pilgrimage to the holy city of Mecca. Hindus hope to escape a cycle of reincarnation and become one with an impersonal, universal spirit through a complex path of exercises and meditation, works, knowledge, devotion – there is no clear concept of salvation or a heaven in Hinduism.

Jesus Christ said he came for a greater purpose than to just teach people how to live good lives. ***He came to die for humanity so we might have eternal life***. His message in his own words was:

The Son of Man came to give his life as a ransom for many.

The Son of Man came to seek and to save that which is lost.

This is my blood of the new covenant which is shed for many for the forgiveness of sins.

It is written: The Christ will suffer and rise from the dead on the third day, and repentance and forgiveness of sins will be preached in his name to all nations. You are witnesses of these things.

John the Baptist said of Jesus, "*Behold the Lamb of God who takes away the sin of the world.*"

For 2,000 years the sacrificial lamb, offered annually on the Jewish Day of Atonement, was only a symbol of God's master plan: the human birth, sinless/perfect life, and sacrificial death of Jesus.

In his letter to the church at Colosse, Paul writes: "*Once you were **alienated** from God. . . but now he has **reconciled** you by Christ's physical body through death.*"

The message of Jesus is God's love letter to all humanity, written in blood as a new covenant or sacred agreement between God and man.

Jesus is the go-between, fully God who emptied himself in obedience and who became a servant, even unto death. He was also fully human, so that his death – not his life or teaching – would provide the just punishment for the sins of the world.

48

The Bible states ***there is no forgiveness without the shedding of blood***. God has built this truth into the fabric of our universe, along with his moral law as contained in the 10 Commandments which He wrote in stone so as to signify their permanence.

When we break God's moral law, we bring His judgment upon ourselves.

God will give to each person according to what he has done.

For God will bring every deed into judgment, including every hidden thing, whether it is good or evil.

Nothing in all creation is hidden from God's sight. Everything is uncovered and laid bare before the eyes of him to whom we must give account.

God tells us that the penalty for our sin – rebellion against His law – is death.

The soul that sins shall die.

We live under a death sentence our entire lives, knowing that like all of our ancestors, we, too, will die. Even though we enjoy a blue sky above us and beautiful green surroundings, we are prisoners awaiting execution, slaves to sin. Our fate will come. The evidence of our guilt will be our death. And when we die, we will stand before the Almighty judge in the courtroom of eternal justice.

The message of Jesus is that we can be saved from what we deserve.

But God demonstrated His own love for us in this: while we were still sinners, Christ died for us.

For God so loved the world, that He gave his one and only son, that whoever believes in Him shall not perish but have eternal life.

In Him we have redemption, through his blood, the forgiveness of sins. . .

Such forgiveness, however, is not automatic for all people everywhere. The second part of Jesus message is this: now that He has died to set all men and women free from sin and eternal death, we must respond in **repentance**.

To repent means to confess and forsake our sins – to do a U-turn away from our sinful behavior and turn to Jesus in faith. It means to stop sinning. It means to willfully choose to live holy lives.

As Jesus began his public teaching his message was clear: "***Repent**, for the kingdom of heaven is near.*"

In Luke 13 his followers asked him about some countrymen who were murdered. His response, "*Unless you **repent**, you too will all perish.*"

Then his disciples asked him about an accident in which 18 men died. Jesus again said, "*Unless you **repent**, you too will all perish.*"

The core of his message has not changed in 2000 years though critics, skeptics, even religious people have tried to change or obscure it:

We were created for eternity, but placed on earth for 70 or so years. We are nurtured in our family, within a community. We were designed to live in peace with each other, to be stewards of the planet, to enjoy fellowship with the Creator God.

But our sins separate us from God and cause crime, wars and every manner of evil.

The message of Jesus runs counter to worldly wisdom: love your enemies and pray for those who persecute you.

The greatest of all must be the servant of all.

Whoever humbles himself will be exalted.

The first shall be last and the last first.

He who loses his life for my sake will gain it.

The message of Jesus, in His own words, is: *"Whoever believes in the Son has eternal life, but whoever rejects the Son will not see life for God's wrath remains on him."*

St. Peter left no doubt about Jesus: ***"Salvation is found in no one else, for there is no other name under heaven given to men by which we must be saved."***

Reasonable Conclusion #4 – the life, death and resurrection of Jesus Christ prove he was unlike any person who ever lived.

5. How Has He Impacted The World?

People are quick to point out that more wars have been fought in the name of religion than for any other reason. Even Karl Marx, who in his youth professed to be a Christian and published his first work, *The Union of the Faithful with Christ*, rejected God, created a secular religion in Communism and called for war against humanity: "We make war against all prevailing ideas of religion, of the state, of country, of patriotism."

Others say Adolf Hitler was a Catholic and lay the Holocaust upon the Christian church's hatred of the Jews. Lest we forget Jesus was a Jew who came for the very purpose of offering his life as a sacrifice for humanity, history records many true Christians who gave their lives in helping Jews escape the Nazis. Read about the life of Corrie Ten Boom and her Dutch family who perished in extermination camps alongside the Jews they loved. Though Hitler was baptized as an infant, one could hardly call him a Christian, a follower of the Prince of Peace, Jesus Christ. He didn't live as a Christian, nor did the Third Reich honor God by the evil it perpetrated.

And then there are the Crusades, the wars fought to regain the holy lands from the infidels. How can Christians deny such an ugly 300 year chapter of world history?

First, not everyone who says he is a Christian really does belong to the church of the Living God as founded by Jesus Christ.

A hypocrite is not a true Christian. He is a pretender, an actor. Hypocrite comes from the Greek word *hypokrisis*, which means playing a part on the stage. A transvestite – a man who dresses up in women's clothes, wear's women's makeup, wigs, jewelry and even adopts female mannerisms and ways of speaking is still a man underneath his disguise – his essential nature remains unchanged, no matter how much he pretends to be a woman.

Jesus said: "*Not everyone who says to me Lord, Lord, will enter the kingdom of heaven, **but only he who does the will of my Father** who is in heaven.*"

What is the will of God the Father? It is to live a holy life and to love each other. (1 Thess 4:7, 9)

Jesus predicted that pretenders doing evil would come in his name – wolves in sheep's clothing. "*Whoever has **my commands and obeys them**, he is the one who loves me.*" (John 14:21)

What are his commands? The greatest command is to love the Lord thy God with all your heart, soul, mind and strength. Part II of the great command is to love your neighbor as much as you love yourself.

Jesus tells his disciples at the last supper, "*A time is coming when anyone who kills you will think he is offering a service to God. They will do such things because they have not known the Father or me.*"

Imposters, pretenders, hypocrites have committed every kind of evil in the name of God. Jesus warned us that not everyone who names the name of Christ is a true follower.

Second, the Crusades had little to do with true Christianity.

According to Ronald C. Finucane, author of *Soldiers of the Faith*, Western Europe during the 10th to the 13th centuries underwent social and political changes that caused so-called Christians to rise up, less for religious fervor and more for economic expansion. To numerous feudal barons and kings, the Near East seemed a bright new world of opportunity: rich lands, greater income, profit, power and prestige. Freeing the Holy Land for all pilgrims – Christian, Jew and Muslim alike -- was often only a noble afterthought.

For the thousands of peasants who joined, the Crusades offered a chance to escape the hopeless bondage of indentured servitude and a chance for adventure, which to ignorant masses, included promises by the Pope of spiritual rewards. "Your bed awaits you in Paradise, should you die in God's service."

More than any other group, the cities of Europe participated for purely economic motives. Venice, Genoa, Vienna, Lyon, London saw the movement as an opportunity to gain commercial bases on the eastern Mediterranean Sea, as well as mercantile privileges from the Muslim lands of the Middle East.

When Pope Urban II, at the Council of Clermont in 1095, initiated the Crusades, he appealed to the courtly love of tournaments and warfare among the barons who had fought each other for hundreds of years. He offered them an opportunity to unite against a common foe which controlled Jerusalem and robbed pilgrims. The Pope also hinted at acquiring lands, wealth and power at the expense of the Arabs and Turks.

Friedrich Heer in *The Medieval World* said, "In every Crusade, and in the individual Crusader, there were conflicting motives connected with religion, economics, politics and class." A 12th Century French poet described Crusaders as "fools, criminals and madmen."

In fact, Professor Kenneth W. Harl of Tulane University suggests the Fourth Crusade was fought between "Christians" from Western Europe against Eastern Orthodox "Christians" over the wealth of Constantinople. After looting the great crossroads city, most Crusaders went home and never even reached the Holy Lands.

54

History views the Crusades as two great Monotheistic religions warring for supremacy, but God's heart must break at what atrocities have been carried out in His holy name.

After the Crusades, the Inquisition, fueled by political alliances between popes and kings, perverted the good news of Jesus Christ and terrorized believers and non-believers alike throughout Europe until the 16th Century. Rather than heed the advice of Bernard of Clairvaux, "Faith is a matter of persuasion, not force," misguided men masquerading as God's agents tortured and executed untold numbers for crimes of heresy or treason against Roman Church teachings.

The Inquisition in Spain, under Torquemada, burned thousands of Jews and Moors who had converted to Christianity, but were unable to change their culture as quickly and thus did not fit into the strict nationalistic policy – despite, according to Heer, "eight centuries of co-existence among Muslims, Jews and Christians." Galileo Galilei, the great Italian astronomer and physicist, though a devout Christian, was found guilty by the Roman Inquisition for supporting Copernicus' views that the earth was not the center of our solar system. Science confirms his beliefs, but the council of Cardinals chose to defend error.

The Salem, Massachusetts witchcraft hysteria of 1692 saw the hanging of 19 purported witches by "good" church people. In the 18th and 19th centuries Colonial expansion often wore the mask of Christian evangelism.

Many atrocious things have been done in the name of God, even in the name of Christianity.

However, these atrocities were not perpetrated by God or His true followers, but by misguided human

55

beings who may have used God as a pretext for their deeds.

In fact, if you examine the atrocities perpetrated by atheists, you find that they killed more people in the last century than all of the crimes of 2000 years of "church" history combined. Communist dictator Joseph Stalin killed 40 million Soviet citizens between 1929 and 1939 because they were not politically correct.

According to the book *China's Bloody Century*, Mao Tse-tung's army killed as many as six million Chinese during the civil war of the 1930s and 1940s (Chiang Kai-shek's Nationalists about 10 million), and another 80 million died between 1950-1976 during the failed Great Leap Forward and Cultural Revolution, according to a 581-page report prepared in 1989 by the official Chinese Academy of Social Sciences for internal use by top Chinese officials.

Pol Pot, the leader of the Marxist regime in Cambodia-Kampuchea, in the 1970's killed two million of his own people. In fact, the Pol Pot regime specifically preached atheism and sought to exterminate all religious expression in Cambodia.

The only war true Christians should fight is a *spiritual war* against Satan for the souls of men and women. Anyone wanting to find examples of those who call themselves Christians, but are, in fact hypocrites, can find history books full of such examples. The true Christian is not necessarily the one who says he is. The true follower of Jesus must produce good fruit.

He or she is the one who does the works Jesus did – acts of love, mercy, kindness and unselfish giving. The man-made, worldly church that meets in a "church" and is a tentacle of a bureaucratic organization is not the same as the transformed body of believers – the true church – which has accomplished much good in the

world.   The first Christian church began as true
followers of Jesus:

*"All the believers were one in heart and mind. No
one claimed that any of his possessions was his own, but
they shared everything they had. There were no needy
persons among them. From time to time those who
owned lands or houses sold them, brought the money
from the sales and put it at the apostles' feet and it was
distributed to anyone if he had need."* (Acts 4:32-35)

Charitable aid for those in need is an important mark
of a Christian. Consider well-known Christian-based
organizations such as the International Red Cross, the
Salvation Army or Habitat for Humanity.

The Red Cross began in Switzerland in 1863, largely
through the efforts of Henry Dunant, the son of devout
Christians. His parents stressed the value of charitable
work. His father helped orphans and parolees; his
mother worked with the sick and poor.

Dunant grew up during the period of religious
awakening known as the *Réveil*, and at age eighteen he
joined the Geneva Society for Alms Giving. In the
following year he founded a group of young men that
met to study the Bible and help the poor, and he spent
much of his free time engaged in prison visits and social
work. In 1852 he founded the Geneva chapter of the
Young Men's Christian Association and three years later
took part in the Paris meeting which founded the
International YMCA.

In 1858 he traveled to Solferino, Italy to appeal to
Napoleon III for fair land and water rights for Algeria,
where he was working. At the time France was fighting
with the Italians against Austria. On the evening of June
24 he witnessed the aftermath of a battle that left 38,000
soldiers injured and dying on the battlefield. Shocked at

such little effort to provide care, he took the initiative to organize the civilian population, especially the women and girls, to provide assistance. They lacked sufficient materials and supplies, so Dunant himself organized the purchase and helped erect makeshift hospitals. He convinced people to service the injured without regard to their side in the conflict as per the slogan "*Tutti fratelli*" -- all are brothers.

So affected by the experience, he wrote *A Memory of Solferino,* published in 1862 at his own expense. He described the battle, its costs, and the chaotic circumstances afterwards. He also developed the idea that in the future a neutral organization should exist to provide care to wounded soldiers. He distributed the book to many leading political and military figures in Europe and then began to travel throughout Europe to promote his ideas. The first meeting of the International Committee of the Red Cross resulted in 1863. A year later the same committee created the Geneva Convention, the basis of International Humanitarian Law. Dunant was awarded the first Nobel Peace Prize in 1901.

Dunant gave God credit for his legacy of charity: "My work was an instrument of His will."

Today the International Red Cross and its sister organization, the Red Crescent, provide relief in 183 countries. In 2004, for example, the ICRC water, sanitation and construction projects met the needs of 20 million people; the ICRC supported hospitals and health-care facilities serving some 2.8 million people; it also provided essential household goods to more than 2.2 million people, food aid to 1.3 million people and assistance to another 1.1 million people in the form of sustainable food-production and micro-economic initiatives.

The American Red Cross annually spends over $3 billion for those in need, all raised by donation. When the 2005 Tsunami devastated Thailand and other Indian Ocean countries, the American Red Cross within weeks raised and sent $110 million for relief services, faster than most governments were able to respond.

The Salvation Army, founded by Christian evangelists Catherine and William Booth in 1865 during the darkest hours of England's Industrial Revolution, emphasizes God's saving love through education, the relief of poverty, and charitable projects. Beginning with the poorest of the poor in London's East End, the Booths opened soup kitchens that led to their and other Christian organizations opening orphanages, clinics, schools and maternity homes.

Operating in 111 countries today, The Salvation Army provides thousands of care facilities and homes for the displaced, street children, elderly, disabled, blind, women in crisis and those disrupted by natural disasters.

The 1879 mission statement in *The Salvationist* magazine emphasized, "We are a salvation people – this is our specialty – getting saved, keeping saved, and then getting somebody else saved." Booth said the ultimate goal was "To subdue a rebellious world to God," and "To challenge the world was right and necessary."

From its earliest days the Army has accorded women equal opportunities, every rank and service being open to them, and from childhood the young are encouraged to love and serve God by serving others. In America the Christmas Red Kettle campaign raises approximately $200 million each year – all of which goes to those in most need.

Habitat for Humanity International is a nonprofit, ecumenical Christian housing ministry founded in 1976 by Linda and Millard Fuller. HFH seeks to eliminate poverty housing and homelessness from the world, and to make decent shelter a matter of conscience and action. Habitat invites people of all backgrounds, races and religions to build houses together in partnership with families in need.

It works through volunteer labor and donations of money and materials. Habitat houses are sold to partner families at no profit, financed with affordable loans. The homeowners' monthly mortgage payments are used to build still more Habitat houses. Habitat is not a giveaway program. In addition to a down payment and the monthly mortgage payments, homeowners invest hundreds of hours of their own labor -- sweat equity -- into building their home and the homes of others.

Fuller has stated: "I see life as both a gift and a responsibility. My responsibility is to use what God has given me to help his people in need."

From humble beginnings in Alabama, Fuller graduated from Auburn University and the University of Alabama Law School. He and a college friend began a marketing firm while still in school. Fuller's business expertise and entrepreneurial drive made him a millionaire at age 29.

But Fuller and his wife decided to sell all of their possessions, give the money to the poor and begin searching for a new focus for their lives. This search led them to Koinonia Farm, a Christian community located near Americus, Ga., where people were looking for practical ways to apply Christ's teachings. In 1973 the Fullers and their four children moved to The Democratic Republic of the Congo (then Zaire) to test their housing model. Their success in Africa encouraged them that they could expand the housing model all over the world.

As of 2005, Habitat has built more than 200,000 houses around the world, providing more than 1,000,000 people in more than 3,000 communities with safe, decent, affordable shelter. Habitat's annual revenues are more than $1 billion.

U.S. President Bill Clinton awarded Fuller the 1996 Presidential Medal of Freedom, the nation's highest civilian honor, calling Habitat "...the most successful continuous community service project in the history of the United States."

Hundreds of other Christian organizations demonstrate God's love to the world by tangible giving.

World Vision began as a Christian relief organization in the 1950s by Dr. Bob Pierce to help children orphaned in the Korean War. It directly aids more than 75 million people worldwide each year, including more than 1 million people in the United States. A total of 2 million children internationally are sponsored by individuals who provide monthly living expenses.

World Vision focuses its work on projects that help communities address the root causes – not just the symptoms – of poverty. In developing countries, World Vision provides food, agricultural training, clean water, primary health care, education, economic development opportunities, and emergency relief. In urban and rural U.S. communities, assistance includes tutoring, mentoring, leadership training, emergency relief, and the provision of building, household and school supplies.

Feed the Children, a Christian relief organization has delivered food, medicine, clothing to families who lack necessities due to famine, war, poverty or natural disaster since 1979. In 2005 Feed The Children shipped 183 million pounds of food and other essentials to children and families in all 50 states and over 100 foreign countries, supplementing more than 1,463,000 meals a day worldwide.

Particular care is given to children who are disabled, homeless or living in the streets. In August 2001, Feed The Children opened the first of what will be a series of Abandoned Baby Centers, which will provide a safe home and family-like environment for abandoned babies and toddlers located near Nairobi, Kenya, to serve childhood victims of the AIDS pandemic.

Four times each year, Feed The Children medical teams travel to developing countries to help people who cannot afford, or who do not have access to, regular medical care. Top priority goes to poor countries that have suffered natural or man-made disasters. In 2004 the Medical Team treated 45,966 patients in medical, eye and dental clinics, and dispensed and filled 58,650 prescriptions for medicine and eyeglasses.

Samaritan's Purse is headed by Franklin Graham, the son of America's best known evangelist, Billy Graham. Like scores of other Christian relief agencies, since 1970 Samaritan's Purse has sent desperately needed food and supplies to the world's destitute – millions of dollars worth donated by other Christians who joyfully obey Jesus' command to feed the hungry, clothe the naked, shelter the homeless and comfort the brokenhearted.

Numerous individuals following in the footsteps of Jesus have had tremendous impact upon the world. **Dr. Albert Schweitzer**, the 1952 Nobel Peace Prize winner, an accomplished musician and theologian, spent most of his life in what is now Gabon, West Africa. After his medical studies in Europe, he went to Africa with his wife to establish a hospital near an already existing mission post. He treated and operated on literally thousands of people. He took care of hundreds of leprosy patients and treated victims of the African sleeping sickness.

As a brilliant young man, who stated in his autobiography, *Out of My Life and Thought,* "Christianity cannot take the place of thought, but it must be founded on it," he faulted Christianity for not putting into action Christ's "great commandment of love and mercy."

Christians had treated this command as a treasured platitude instead of using it as a basis "for opposing slavery, witch burning, torture, and all the other ancient and medieval forms of inhumanity."

He also faulted Christians for ignoring the reality of the Lord's Prayer: "Only a Christianity which is ruled by the idea and intent of the Kingdom of God, is genuine. Only such a Christianity can give to the world what it so desperately needs."

This Kingdom of God on earth was the goal towards which Christ taught his followers to work and pray. A world in which God's will would be "done on earth, as it is in heaven" was a world in which compassion, kindness and love were the rule.

The Albert Schweitzer Society is still an active force that continues his work in 25 countries and ministers to "the poor, sick, lepers, and all those suffering from injustice due to race, sex, color and creed."

Mother Teresa of Calcutta, India, an Albanian nun who founded the Missionaries for Charity was also awarded the Nobel Prize (1979). In 1946, by her own account, she received a calling from God "to serve Him among the poorest of the poor." She said, "I see God in every human being. When I wash the leper's wounds, I feel I am nursing the Lord himself. Is it not a beautiful experience?"

She started an open-air school for homeless children and was soon joined by voluntary helpers. She received financial support from church organizations and the municipal authorities. In 1949, some of her former pupils joined her. They found men, women, and children dying on the streets who were rejected by local hospitals. The group rented a room so they could care for helpless people otherwise condemned to die in the gutter.

Her order which began with 12 members today has more than 4,000 nuns running orphanages, AIDS hospices, charity centers worldwide, and caring for refugees, the blind, disabled, aged, alcoholics, the poor and homeless and victims of floods, epidemics and famine on six continents.

Many of the first hospitals begun in the poor and developing countries of Asia, Africa and Latin America were started by Christians. Hospital comes from Latin *hospes* (host), which is also the root for the words hotel and hospitality.

The Council of Nicaea in 325 A.D. urged the Church to provide for the poor, sick, widows and strangers. It ordered the construction of a hospital in every cathedral town. Among the earliest were those built by the physician Saint Sampson in Constantinople and by Basil, bishop of Caesarea. The latter was attached to a monastery and provided lodgings for poor and travelers, as well as treating the sick and infirm. There was a separate section for lepers.

Medieval hospitals in Europe were religious communities with care provided by monks and nuns. An old French term for hospital is hôtel-Dieu, "hostel of God." Some were attached to monasteries. Others were independent and had their own endowments, usually of property, which provided income for their support. Some were multi-function. Others were founded specifically as leper hospitals, or as refuges for the poor or pilgrims.

Many of the first schools were started by Christians who pioneered education, especially for girls and women. The Greeks and Romans before Christ only educated boys and men, but Christian doctrine teaches gender, racial and ethnic equality.

Today's higher education directly traces its roots to medieval European Scholasticism. *Schola,* Latin for school, referred to the cathedral and abbey schools which developed into the first modern universities.

In the 2nd Century Justin Martyr established schools in Ephesus and Rome. Clement established a well-known school in Alexandria which produced prominent Christian leaders such as Origen and Athanasius. The school taught doctrine, mathematics, medicine and grammar.

By the 4th Century cathedral schools, maintained by schola(r)-monks and clergy, added Christian doctrine, grammar, rhetoric, logic, arithmetic, music, geometry and astronomy.

The first modern university, the University of Paris, began about 1150, attached to the cathedral on the ile de La Cite. Then Oxford began in 1167 and Cambridge in 1200. The first deputies of Oxford declared the institution *Schola secunda ecclesiae*, the second school of the Church, of which Paris was the first. Theology was the primary subject taught by the resident Dominican, Franciscan and Benedictine religious orders.

Many European and Asian Universities were founded by Christians. The prestigious Hong Kong University was founded by the London Missionary Society in 1887. The University of Nanking (金陵大學) was begun in 1888 by missionary C.H. Fouler. It merged with Nanjing University (南京大學) in 1952. Suzhou University (苏州大学) was started by Christians in 1900.

In 1919 Beijing's notable Yenching University (燕京大学) integrated three Christian universities founded by missionaries in the 19th century into one.

65

President John Leighton Stuart raised funds through international donors to buy the Qing Dynasty Royal Gardens to build a scenic campus which was completed in 1926. Theology, Law and Medicine were the main schools, with additional studies in Arts and Sciences. The Harvard-Yenching Institute was jointly founded in 1928 by Yenching University and Harvard for the *education of humanity* in East Asia.

After the People's Republic was established in 1949, the Christian Yenching University merged with Peking University (北京大学), and in 1952 Peking University moved from central Beijing to its present Yenching campus.

In America, in 1636, seven years after the Puritans established the Massachusetts Bay Colony as a Beacon on the Hill in Boston, thirty-one year old clergyman John Harvard, who lay dying, donated his 400-book library and half his property (779 pounds) for an institution to educate Christian ministers. Harvard's historic mottos on the university seals are *In Christi Glorium,* to the glory of Christ, and *Christo et Ecclesiae,* for Christ and the Church. The 1636 rules of **Harvard** declared:

"Let every student be plainly instructed and earnestly pressed to consider well, the main end of his life and studies is, to know God and Jesus Christ, which is eternal life, (John 17:3); and therefore to lay Jesus Christ as the only foundation of all sound knowledge and learning. And seeing the Lord only giveth wisdom, let everyone seriously set himself by prayer in secret to seek it of him (Proverbs 2:3)."

Early Harvard alumni include John Adams, Samuel Adams, John Hancock, Josiah Quincy and James Otis.

The second American university, **William and Mary** (1693), began, as stated in its charter,

that the Church of Virginia may be furnished with a seminary of ministers of the Gospel, and that the youth may be piously educated in good letters and manners, and that the Christian faith may be propagated. . .

William and Mary graduates include Thomas Jefferson, James Monroe and John Marshall, Supreme Court Chief Justice.

Yale University was founded in 1701 by ten Connecticut clergymen for ministerial training. The trustees purpose was "to plant and under ye Divine blessing to propagate in this Wilderness, the blessed Reformed, Protestant Religion, in ye purity of its Order and Worship." Students studied theology, as well as Hebrew, Greek and Latin to better master the Scriptures.

Yale grads include patriot Nathan Hale, who said before being hanged by the British," I only regret that I have but one life to lose for my country"; also inventor Eli Whitney and author of the first American dictionary, Noah Webster, who said, "No truth is more evident to my mind than that the Christian religion must be the basis of any government intended to secure the rights and privileges of a free people."

Dartmouth College grew out of the home and efforts of the Reverend Eleazer Wheelock (a Yale graduate) in 1775 to train young ministers to Christianize the New England Indian tribal groups. **Columbia** was founded by royal charter in 1754 in the Trinity Church schoolhouse to provide a Christian institution in New York City. Its early grads include Alexander Hamilton and John Jay.

The College of New Jersey, now known as **Princeton** University, was founded as a ministerial training school for Presbyterians during the Great

Religious Awakening early in the 18th Century. The University of **Pennsylvania** grew from the Charity School established in 1740 by Christian evangelist George Whitefield. **Brown** University was chartered as Rhode Island College in 1764 by Baptist descendants of Roger Williams "to train ministers and to educate youth properly in the Christian faith." **Rutgers** was created in 1776 by members of the Dutch Reformed Church to provide "the strictest regard to moral conduct and especially that young men of suitable abilities may be instructed in divinity."

Thomas Hopkins Gallaudet, a Congregational clergyman, often credited as the father of American Sign Language, opened the first school for the deaf in the USA in 1817. In 1857, Gallaudet's youngest son, Edward Miner Gallaudet, became president of what would become the world's first and still most prominent college for deaf students, **Gallaudet** University in Washington D.C.

Most of the first universities in America were distinctly Christian.

Many founders of the American Republic graduated from these schools. Forty-three of the 56 signers of The Declaration of Independence were avowed Christians. They refer to God in the very first sentence of the Declaration. The second sentence states these famous words: *"We hold these truths to be self-evident that all men are created equal, that they are endowed **by their Creator** with certain unalienable Rights, that among these are Life, Liberty and the Pursuit of Happiness.*

Patrick Henry, known as the firebrand of the American Revolution, is still remembered for his words, "Give me liberty or give me death." But the context of these words is often deleted. Here is what precedes his famous quote of March 23, 1775, at St.

John's Church in Richmond as he urged his fellow Virginians to arm in self-defense:

"An appeal to arms and the God of hosts is all that is left us . . . we shall not fight our battles alone. There is a just God that presides over the destinies of nations . . .The battle sir, is not of the strong alone. . . Is life so dear or peace so sweet as to be purchased at the price of chains and slavery? Forbid it, Almighty God! I know not what course others may take; but as for me, give me liberty, or give me death!"

Consider these words from George Washington, Father of the Nation, in his Inaugural Address of 1789, *"It would be peculiarly improper to omit in this first official act my fervent supplication to that Almighty Being who rules over the universe, who presides in the councils of nations, and whose providential aids can supply every human defect"*

And then in the first official, national Thanksgiving Day Proclamation that same year: "*Whereas it is the duty of all Nations to acknowledge the **providence of Almighty God**, to obey his will, to be grateful for his benefits, and humbly to implore his protection and favor. . . "*

Inscribed on the east face of the aluminum apex which crowns the Washington Monument, by law the tallest building in Washington D.C., at 555 feet overlooking the nation's capitol, are the words "*Laus Deo*," – meaning, "Praise God."

At Washington's Mount Vernon tomb above the iron door of the inner vault on inset stone are the words from St. John's Gospel: "I am the Resurrection and the Life; he that believeth in Me, though he were dead, yet shall he live."

69

Second President John Adams, in a June 28, 1813 letter to Thomas Jefferson wrote, "*The general principles upon which the Fathers achieved independence were the general principles of Christianity...I will avow that I believed and now believe that those general principles of Christianity are as eternal and immutable as the existence and the attributes of God.*"

Third President Thomas Jefferson, usually considered to be a Deist, wrote in a letter in 1803: "*I am a Christian, in the only sense in which he (Jesus) wished any one to be; sincerely attached to his doctrines, in preference to all others.*"

In fact, Jefferson thought Christianity so important that he personally authored a work for the Indians entitled *The Life and Morals of Jesus of Nazareth* which set forth the teachings of Jesus as delivered in the Gospels. The 57th Congress reprinted the book in 1903 and for many years copies were given to new members.

Fourth President James Madison and architect of the U.S. Constitution said in 1778 to the General Assembly of Virginia, "*We have staked the whole future of American civilization, not upon the power of government, far from it. We've staked the future of all our political institutions upon our capacity...to sustain ourselves according to the Ten Commandments of God.*"

At the Constitutional Convention of 1787, Madison proposed the plan to divide the central government into three branches – Judicial, Legislative and Executive. The separation of powers or *trias politica*, a term coined by French philosopher Baron Charles Montesquieu, was developed by Madison in Federalist Paper 51. His inspiration for this model of government came from the Perfect Governor, as he read Isaiah

70

*33:22: "For the LORD is our **judge**, the LORD is our **lawgiver**, the LORD is our **king**; He will save us."*

In 1781 Robert Aitken, publisher of *The Pennsylvania Magazine* and official printer of the first Journals of the U.S. Congress, petitioned Congress to authorize and if possible fund the printing of a complete Bible in the English language to meet the shortage of scriptures.

On September 10, 1782, the United States Congress did authorize Aitken -- the only instance in history of Congress authorizing the printing of a Bible. In 1783, George Washington wrote a letter commending Aitken for his Bible which today is known as the "Bible of the American Revolution" and remains one of the most rare and valuable of early American Bibles.

Benjamin Franklin, Alexander Hamilton, John Hancock, John Jay – and every U.S. president – have publicly recognized that America's destiny is the result of a covenant relationship with Almighty God beginning in 1620 when the Pilgrims signed the Mayflower Compact off Plymouth Rock.

"Having undertaken for the Glory of God, and Advancement of the Christian Faith. . ."

The U.S. Census Bureau in 2002 concluded that eight of ten Americans identify themselves as Christians. Worldwide in 2005, according to the Encyclopedia Britannica statistical research service, *2.1 billion people* follow Jesus Christ -- almost 40 percent of the earth's population.

Reasonable Conclusion #5 – For 2000 years Jesus Christ and his body the Church has had and continues to have a profound impact upon the world.

6. Does He Transform Individual Lives?

Lynn's Story

My father took his own life when I was a 17-year-old high school senior.

The Bible offers comfort to those who struggle with life's difficult events in a passage found in Romans 8:28:

"And we know that all things work together for good to those who love God and who are the called according to His purpose."

But on the morning my mother found my father dead in our garage from carbon monoxide, I would have screamed in anger at anyone who had tried to comfort me with that scripture. "What kind of God allows such things to happen? Don't tell me to love a God who let my father die! I prayed to God to help my family and He abandoned us!"

My father's tragic death caused me to reject everything I believed in and valued. I tumbled into a tailspin of anger, depression, rebellion and self-hatred which nearly cost me my life.

My Beginning

I was raised in a family that believed in God and went to church. When I was a little girl God was an important part of my life. Along with my sisters and brother, I attended Sunday school, summer Bible camp, sang in the youth choir, was confirmed and participated in youth activities at our small Lutheran church. My parents' attended regularly and financially supported the church.

As a child I was spellbound by the stories visiting missionaries told. The color slides and 8mm films told of suffering people in faraway Africa and Asia, and touched my heart. I vowed one day I would go to those places to help those people. That was a secret desire I kept in my heart and never told anyone until much later.

When I was about 11 my father lost his job. By then there were five children to feed and clothe. We struggled for a time, but my parents worked hard to provide what we needed.

My mom was always a great cook who made salads and pies at home to sell to local stores and restaurants. I never considered then how much they must have struggled, but eventually my dad got a better job with a higher salary. One of the sacrifices he had to make in his job, however, was to travel away from home all week.

Dad's new job allowed us to move into a bigger home in a nicer neighborhood. My parents had only drunk beer occasionally, but now they began to drink martinis in the evenings. Like other upwardly mobile couples at the time, they would have a cocktail before dinner, but it wasn't long before one cocktail became several. Then my parents began to drink heavily on weekends, especially my mother.

When Dad came home on Fridays, mom was ready to go out and have some fun. She had been left all week to take care of our home and us kids and she felt she deserved an escape. But Dad, who'd been gone all week wanted to stay home, relax and eat my mother's good cooking. Occasionally he would take my mother out to dinner and dancing, but mostly they just stayed home and drank -- then ended up arguing a lot.

Over time the arguments became abusive. My mother's violent temper often instigated the physical violence. Once in a rage my mother attacked my father. To protect himself he put his hands up and pushed her away. She lost her balance and crashed through a glass window that separated our family room and kitchen – breaking several ribs and cutting her face seriously enough to require stitches. She lied to our family doctor that she had fallen into the window while hanging curtains.

My mother had grown up in an abusive family and was often been beaten by her father when he was drunk. Now she was becoming just like him.

Many weekend nights I lay in bed unable to sleep because of their fights. I prayed they would stop. I even prayed that God would cause my mother to die, because I felt the fights were her fault because she was the violent one. But then I prayed again and asked God to forgive me. I begged Him for the fighting to stop. It only got worse.

Soon mom began to drink every day. Sometimes she would pass out with the TV on and cigarettes burning in ashtrays. I would lay awake and wait until she was asleep and then go put out her cigarettes. I was terrified she would burn the house down.

I grew ashamed of my parents. They would stop drinking for awhile, and then life would almost seem normal. But it never lasted. I remained active in the church until high school. But gradually I stopped going. My parents never went except on holidays or when one of us got confirmed. They didn't seem to care if we kids went so we didn't.

I made new friends in high school and was in speech and drama, student government and school clubs. I attended school dances, athletic events and was a good student despite the problems at home.

Because I now had more freedom to go out, I began to lie to my parents about where I went and with whom. I started smoking with my friends. I didn't care. After all, who were my parents to tell me what to do? They smoked, got drunk and fought all the time -- why shouldn't I do what I wanted?

We tried to act like a normal family by taking summer vacations. But they were torturous. My parents went out at night with neighbors at the resort but came back fighting and drunk. I hated to go anywhere with them.

I attended meetings for children of alcoholics. At first I did this secretly, but the counselors encouraged us to be truthful about attending so we would not "enable" our parents' behavior. When I told my parents, they made me stop going.

Months before my father's death, I resolved I would never go anywhere again with my parents when they were drinking. I was stubborn about this, and my attitude got me into trouble with my parents, but they couldn't force me to go, even when they would yell and ground me to my room.

My senior year I noticed a change in my dad. He became quiet and withdrawn. My mother would try to goad him into fighting, but he would refuse to speak to her. Sometimes he would walk out of the house and come back later after she had passed out. I was worried about him.

On New Year's Eve --13 days before he committed suicide -- as my sister and I prepared to go out for the evening, my father did something out of character. He kissed each of us gently on the cheek. He hugged us and told us he loved us. I had rarely heard him say that. Though he was affectionate with us when we were little, sadly, he rarely touched us after we became teenagers. He seemed calm, clear-headed, and he

75

wasn't drunk. I wanted to feel good about his surprising affection, but I sensed that something bad was about to happen.

I went to the pastor of our church. I barely knew this man, and he had never come to our home to visit. He was soft-spoken, a man of God, so I believed.

I thought I could trust him. I poured out my heart. I told of my family's problems, my parents' alcoholism and violence. I begged him to help us before something terrible happened. Before I left his office, I pleaded with him to talk to my parents, but to not tell them I had come. I knew how much they tried to hide their problems.

I walked home in the January cold. By the time I got to our front door, my parents knew everything! The pastor had called my parents immediately after I left and told them what I had shared in confidence. They were furious!

My mother screamed at me, "How dare you tell other people about what happens in this family! We will take care of our problems ourselves. We don't need anyone to get involved."

I remember feeling physically ill that a man of God had betrayed my trust. I was even angry at God and wanted nothing to do with Him. Where was He the past seven years since my parents started drinking and fighting? I prayed, but where was He? Would a loving God allow this pain? Would He remain silent while my family self-destructed? I couldn't trust the pastor and I couldn't trust God. So I quit praying.

A week later my father killed himself.

We were awakened early January 13 by my mother's screams. Sirens and red flashing lights whirred outside our bedroom window. I lay in bed next to my older sister in the dormitory-sized bedroom we shared with our two younger sisters. We were all awake, but frozen with fear, unable to say anything. I wonder to this day what it was like for my brother who had his own bedroom. He must have felt lonely and frightened.

We were suddenly blinded by the overhead light. My poor uncle had come to tell us: "Girls, your dad has passed away." His words were slow and choked. The shock of hearing those words has remained in my mind.

Your dad has passed away. Your dad has passed away. It was too unreal.

At my father's funeral I sat stiffly on the front pew of the church and glared at the pastor. How dare he give the eulogy for a man he never bothered to help. He didn't even know my father. What right did he have to say anything about my father? I have no idea what he said. I hated him! I hated God! What had he ever done for me or for my family? From that point on I swore I would never go to church again.

A few nights after his funeral, my father appeared to me as I lie in bed. He looked so real I could have touched him. He said, "Look after your mother." Then he was gone.

Was it a dream? I wasn't afraid. Do the dead come back to tell us things? Was he a ghost? Because of this eerie visitation I began to explore the occult.

I spent hours in the library reading books by authors like Edgar Cayce, a well known occult writer. Because I rejected Christianity, I began to look into other religions like Hinduism and Buddhism. Maybe I could work out my bad karma now and be reborn into a higher state of consciousness.

In spite of my family tragedy, I maintained good grades and no one except my closest friends knew the turmoil inside me.

My mom took Valium to help her through my dad's death. She became addicted. When she wasn't numbed by Valium, she drank herself into oblivion. Every night she would walk around the house with a drink in hand, babbling incoherently. My siblings and I learned to tune her out. We sat in front of the TV and tried not to listen to her angry ramblings. We adapted to this bizarre way of life in order to survive.

A part of me still wanted to please her. I thought if only I could be good enough, she would be okay. I mostly wanted to do well in school so I could go to college to escape the madness at home.

My older sister was already living on campus, and I spent as much time with her as I could. I graduated, got a summer job and on weekends hung out with my best friend. We pretended we were already college coeds.

I often spent the night at her house. Sometimes we would drink wine—her mother was thoroughly modern—and would drink with us. We'd put on our makeup, dress provocatively, grab our cigarettes and go out. Once at the hangouts, I would smoke, laugh loudly and curse like I thought a college girl should to get guys to notice me. I was always small and thin, so I probably looked like a 12- year-old playing dress up. But guys never noticed my skinny, boyish body.

Aside from depression, I also fell into anorexic eating behavior and became obsessed with the possibility that I might get fat. My self esteem plummeted.

I began to suffer bouts of suicidal depression which I was usually able to overcome. College would get me away from mom's drinking and tirades. I dreamed of becoming a journalist who traveled the world and wrote about what she saw. This dream helped me conquer the darkness that threatened to envelop me.

But I was still haunted my father's command to *look after your mother.*

Dark thoughts haunted me even more. I hated my mother, then felt guilty for thinking that. I'd wish she would die. Then I'd wish I would die. I was so confused. I thought I hated God and sometimes I told Him so.

I expected that one day He would strike me dead for my blasphemy.

The summer after I graduated, while my mom was at work, a friend who also had family problems frequently came over and we'd take out my Ouija Board. We'd consult it for guidance about our futures. At first it was fun. We'd laugh and accuse each other of moving the *planchette.* We shared with each other what we had been reading in various occult books. We felt this gave us a sense of power and control in our lives.

One day we asked the board who we were talking to. The *planchette* began to spell very slowly, G – O, but then stopped for a long while. Suddenly it moved crazily all over the board and spelled out the word S-A-T-A-N.

We stopped immediately and she said she had to go home. I put the board away and we never played with it again. The experience terrified me. I thought I didn't believe in the devil. When I was confirmed in the Lutheran church I said, "I renounce the devil and all his works and ways." But they were merely words I recited after the pastor.

My interest in the occult began to wane. I turned my attention to beginning college in the fall.

New Beginnings

79

On the second day of college my life changed forever. I met Michael, the man I would marry two years later. He was the most gentle, soft spoken, handsome young man I had ever met. What was best of all . . . he was as attracted to me as I was to him.

Michael was the oldest son in a large Catholic family. He wrote poems to me. For a girl of 17 to meet a poet who is in love with you must be the most romantic thing imaginable, I thought. After a two year courtship, we became engaged and announced to our parents we would marry during the summer between our sophomore and junior years. He was 20, I was only 19. His parents were not thrilled about the timing and wanted us to wait, but they wouldn't stand in the way. His mother knew how in love we were and was supportive of us.

My mother was absolutely opposed. She refused to discuss it. I was devastated. But Michael went to my mother, who herself had recently remarried and only a little over a year after my father's death (to a man we all detested). He told her we would be married and that we hoped she would come to wedding. She didn't have to help us in any way -- we were planning the wedding and paying for it ourselves.

A few days before the wedding, my mother came to my grandmother's where I was staying. She asked if there was anything we needed and could she host a rehearsal dinner for us? Our wedding was small, so there was really nothing she could do. I told her to just come and enjoy herself; the wedding reception was to be held at Michael's parents' house. I remember how quiet and sad she seemed. I felt genuinely sorry; her stubbornness had spoiled what should have been the happiest day of my life.

I began to see her differently: what a sad, lonely woman she was. I reasoned she had done it to herself.

But I remained unforgiving toward her. I felt she was largely responsible for my dad's death — she and God. I couldn't bring myself to forgive either one of them.

We married in the Catholic Church even though I wasn't Catholic. The service was brief, but we did say our vows to remain faithful in sickness and in health, for richer, for poorer, for better or for worse, so help us God. As married college students, we would be poor; and with my troubled past, I would definitely test Michael's patience.

I was so insecure after a year of marriage that I began to have doubts about Michael's love and faithfulness. I was jealous and would fly into rages anytime he talked to another young woman. I frequently ranted and threw things at him. I tried to strike him sometimes. I accused him of having an affair. In depression and anger I took a hair barrette and scraped my arms, causing bruising and bleeding.

Michael was patient, but extremely concerned. He knew how difficult my life had been growing up in an alcoholic family with physical and verbal abuse. He urged me to seek counseling. But I told him I could get through this myself. Actually, I was too proud to admit I needed help. After some terrible fights during the first year, I often felt foolish and asked him to forgive me, which he did—over and over again. He told me, "It's okay. You don't have to apologize." This made me feel even more guilt.

When we graduated and got teaching jobs, I had fewer bouts of anger. But thoughts of suicide still plagued me. I often had an inner battle going on that not even my husband knew about.

Over the years, I felt self-recrimination and bitterness. Sometimes when I was alone I would cry uncontrollably and ask my father, "Why did you do that to our family? How could you abandon your children that way?" Then I would turn on God, "If you are so loving, how could you let all these terrible things happen? Why didn't you stop it? I always tried to be good, but why do you hate me so much, God?"

I tried not to visit my mother. If she called and was drunk, I would hang up. I told her I would never talk if she was drinking. I felt this was a good way to help her face her problem—after all, I wasn't about to enable that behavior. But I felt little love or compassion for her, only anger and bitterness. I never saw my own hypocrisy. I expected her to get help when I refused to get help myself.

After we had been married for 6 years, we began to think about a family. I knew Michael would be a great father, but I wasn't sure I would be a good mother. I was afraid I would be like my own mother -- abusive and impatient. I had doubts that this would be a good thing for us to do. We decided our children should be raised Catholic.

Even though I had no real interest in becoming a Catholic, I began to take classes. Father Joe was open minded and relaxed, and I enjoyed talking with him. At the time we were teaching at the Catholic high school my husband had graduated from. Many of the teachers had become friends. One young woman in particular, Sister Nancy, always glowed with love and energy. I often thought, "I wish I could be like her. I wish people would see me the way I see her – kind, loving and accepting."

Father Joe didn't choose the traditional catechism for me. He knew I understood Catholic doctrine and tradition. I had taken classes years ago when Michael and I became engaged. My Lutheran background caused me to have some doctrinal sticking points, but Father Joe ignored those and moved to the heart of the matter: "Who is Jesus?"

The first book he wanted me to read was the gospel of John in the New Testament. I thought I knew this gospel…but this time the words weren't so difficult to comprehend. The message became very clear to me:

"For God so loved the world that he gave His only begotten Son, that whoever believes in Him should not perish but have everlasting life. For God did not send His Son into the world to condemn the world, but that the world through Him might be saved."

"There is now therefore no condemnation for those who are in Christ Jesus."

As I continued to study and have discussions with Father Joe, Jesus became real to me. I began to go to mass every day. I wasn't confirmed as a Catholic yet, so I couldn't take communion. But when I took communion years before as a Lutheran, it meant very little.

I realized that what made the difference was that now I understood the true message of the gospel…God so loved me, Lynn, that He sent Jesus to die for me, to set me free from the power of sin and death. And his death was so painful, so bloody, and yet He willingly endured it for me. For me!

I began to feel the presence of God in my life in a way I had never known. I couldn't wait to get to school so I could go to morning mass and listen to the words of God being read, and sometimes even I got to read those words during the service. God's word became real and was food for my hungry, tormented soul.

I was confirmed into the Catholic Church on November 1 – All Saints Day at a special mass held in the school auditorium. As a hopeless sinner, I understood my need to repent and trust in Jesus. When my name was called to celebrate my first communion with my husband, my students and my school "family," I was overwhelmed by the joy and peace of the Lord's presence. I could almost audibly hear Him say, "You are my beloved daughter in whom I am well pleased." Christ had become real and I now understood that He had died to set all the captives free — that complete freedom would come to me a few months later.

Life was good . . . for a time. On June 17th our first son Aeron Michael came home to us. He was beautiful! When we took him to show my mother, she wept in joy to see him. She said, "Lynn, he looks just like you did when you were a baby!" And he did! One of God's greatest miracles came home to be with us that day — our first son.

We began to read the Bible regularly and attend church and prayer meetings. At first the glow of my re-found faith in God was enough, but soon feelings of darkness and depression began to creep in.

In our prayer group we had several mature Christians who had talked about spiritual bondage. Two of the leaders of the group were parents to a girl who was a student at the high school. She had become more irrational over the past several months and her behavior became so impossible her parents committed her to the mental health ward of the local hospital. One night a group of four people, including her parents, went to her room, prayed with her and she was set free from several demonic spirits.

The girl's change was evident immediately. Her skin cleared up overnight and her hair, which had been an oily, dirty blond became a silky, pure white blond. Her dark, unfocused eyes sparkled clear and blue. She became a top student artist and an outspoken witness for what Jesus had done for her. She shared with other students about her miracle of deliverance and salvation in Christ. A revival spread among the students as more and more personally encountered Jesus Christ.

I knew all this and was amazed and overjoyed for the family. But I needed help. An evil presence enveloped my mind and often spoke to me that I was worthless and a terrible mother. I would probably ruin my son's life. I decided I had to end my life before I destroyed my son's and my husband's happiness. I searched in vain through our home to find something with which to take my life. I was frantic. But through this fog of insanity, I decided I needed to call my friend, the mother of the girl who had been set free.

When she answered the phone, I told her what was happening and she prayed immediately with me and bound a spirit of suicide. I felt at peace. But I knew this was not over. We scheduled a time to meet at the home of a prayer group member. A prayer team was arranged for me.

On the night scheduled, I was ready. I had prayed all day and asked God to free me. I didn't want to be in chains of darkness anymore. I wanted to be happy and joyful as I remembered being as a child. My mother had once told me I was her happiest baby. But life had allowed the enemy to "come in like a flood" -- to try to destroy me as he had my father and mother.

That night as friends prayed, they looked into my eyes and ordered the demons to release me. Suddenly, I felt I would explode. I began to scream – long, shrill howls. In my mind I was thinking, "What is this? This isn't me. Get out you, get out!"

After a few moments an all-enveloping warmth swept through my body, and I began to laugh out loud and sing and praise God. All those years of bondage were over. I felt free.

I was free.

As I drove home that night I continued to sing and praise God. I could hardly wait to tell Michael. When I did, he was incredulous. He couldn't believe it. Later he admitted to me that he kept waiting for the dark cloud to return, but it never did. Praise God -- it never did.

Over time, as God healed my inner wounds, I learned to see my mother as God saw her. I was at last able to forgive her and mend our relationship. A year before she died, too young, due to the damage years of alcohol and drugs had inflicted upon her body, she also came to see her need for a Savior. She went around to her family and children to seek forgiveness. And then she went on to her heavenly home.

Now I am the mother of two wonderful grown sons. Two years ago my dream of becoming a missionary did come true. We spent one year in China teaching and sharing the gospel with our students and our colleagues. We plan to return. We will continue to go wherever the Lord sends us, no matter what the cost.

By telling my story, I hope to convince others of what I ultimately came to realize: that God is there for us even when we don't think He is. God never gave up on this "prodigal" daughter. I still don't always know why God allows some evil things to happen, but I do know we have a spiritual enemy who is at work all day, every day to try to kill, steal from and destroy human beings.

But now I know how to battle him and who to go to for help! We are to do the works Jesus did and set the captives free! Deliverance is the children's bread -- for all who believe.

Reasonable conclusion #6 -- Though over two billion people follow Jesus worldwide, almost every single person can testify how God has changed his or her life.

7. What Then Must We Do?

The world mistakenly sees Christianity as a religion, a "Western" system of dogma, an alternative to Buddhism or Islam. The world views Jesus as a peer to Buddha and Mohammed. Many think Jesus failed because he died.

But the core tenet of Christianity is that ***each individual must enter into a personal relationship with the one and only, Living Creator God through repentance and faith***.

To be a Christ-*ian* means to be a follower of Jesus the "Christ" – Hebrew for "Messiah," or Greek "Anointed One." Christ is not his last name.

Jesus, the eternal **Word** of John's gospel, became a man to reveal through his death God's love for all humanity. . . for all time. . . to every nation and people:

*"In the beginning was the Word and the Word was with God and **the Word was God**. He was with God in the beginning.*

"Through him all things were made; without him nothing was made that has been made. In him was life and that life was the light of men. The light shines in the darkness but the darkness has not understood it.

*The **Word became flesh** and made his dwelling among us."*

Jesus was God/man – a paradox in human logic. He came to *die* to bring *life*—another seeming contradiction. Jesus, the world's Savior, becomes savior to each person who must receive him as savior. He taught that all who follow him are adopted into God's family; the Heavenly Father becomes our Father. The Holy Spirit – who is, in essence, *spirit* – becomes a spiritual life force in every believer.

Thus, Jesus is not just another holy man or religious guru. He is the one, true, living God who solved the dilemma no human could: how to overcome sin which leads to death.

His crucifixion was the only solution – a sacrificial death as our atonement.

When God the Father placed all of the moral evil, filth and sin of the world – along with His own wrath because of our sins – upon a perfect, sinless man who was God the Son, He made forgiveness and reconciliation possible for every human being.

We sinned; Jesus died in our place.

But forgiveness is not automatic. Jesus died for the sin of the world – true. But each person must stand alone before the judge of the universe in the court of eternal justice and give an account for him or herself. Every moment of our life will be laid bare.

If we could access our memories like a computer hard drive and replay every secret thought we ever had, every word we have spoken, every single thing we ever did, and then honestly judge ourselves as a good or bad person – what would be our verdict?

"Most people will proclaim their own goodness." (Proverbs 20:6)

We may not be a Mother Teresa, but we are as good as our neighbor, right? We are better than many in prison, right? Most people rate themselves above average.

As an experiment, we have often asked our students at the end of a semester to grade themselves. No one ever gives him or herself a C. A few will give themselves a B. The majority think they deserve an A when, in truth and according to the grade book, they do not. We judge ourselves by our human standards.

But God will judge us by his holy, perfect standard because He is a holy, perfect God. Jesus is His standard.

In our ignorance, in our arrogance, in our foolishness we think God will let us slip into heaven under his perfect moral law because we are "good enough," or "not that bad."

Hitler will go to hell. That's our standard. Because we never committed murder we deserve heaven. We assume wrongly that God will grade on the curve. Don't we all rank ourselves above average? But self-pride blinds us to the truth.

I, the Jury: judge yourself. Apply God's criteria of goodness to your personal, historical record.

"*Nothing in all creation is hidden from God's sight. Everything is uncovered and laid bare before the eyes of him to whom we must give account.*" (Hebrews 4:13)

How do you measure up against God's moral law, the 10 Commandments?

I. "You shall have no other gods before me."

This command doesn't just mean to not worship gods other than the One, True God of the Bible. We must also do something. We must put God first in our life. Is He our first thought every morning, our last thought at night? Do we think about Him constantly throughout the day? Do we bless his goodness before every meal? Do we thank Him for every breath we take and for every beat of our heart?

Jesus rephrased this commandment: "*You shall love the Lord, your God, with all your heart, mind, soul and strength.*" Every fiber of our being must honor Him who gives us life. Psalm 14 says we are all guilty of breaking this command: There is no one who does good, no one who seeks God. Punishment: death.

II. The second command is similar to the first: *"You shall not make for yourself any graven image."*

Worshipping statues or stone idols made by men is foolish, but this command also implies an idol we invent in our minds to suit ourselves. To me, my god would not condemn people to hell. My god is all loving. My god accepts me just the way I am. My god overlooks my failings. Unfortunately, such a false god exists only in someone's imagination.

An idol can also be anything we devote more time or energy to than the one, true God -- our career, our family, sports or hobbies, another person, money or worldly success. We are warned not to love the created world more than the Creator.

Ask yourself: what is the most important thing in your life? If you say your health or your career or anything but your relationship with God is foremost, then you need to re-check your priorities. If your relationship with God does not come first, you might be placing an idol above Him.

III. *"You shall not take the name of the Lord your God in vain."*

We think words are only words and an occasional curse word is justified or to swear when you bang your finger with a hammer is not so bad because everyone does it. By our human standards, to use the Savior's name in anger or say God and damn together is normal and natural.

But the name above every other name should be so highly esteemed that we should never drag it through the mud by careless use.

90

When we do we defame the God who gave us life. Pious Jews were forbidden to even speak God's name aloud.

But today in casual conversation, in the media, from the mouths of young children we hear and tolerate profanity. God will not be mocked. He will hold each of us accountable for misusing his name.

In vain means "devoid of value."

IV. "Remember to keep the Sabbath holy."

For the Jews, Sabbath is traditionally from Friday at sunset to Saturday at sunset. For the Christian, because we celebrate Jesus' resurrection to life on the first day of the week, most Christians honor God on Sunday.

The letter of the law is not whether Saturday or Sunday is the correct day of worship, but the intent of the law is that God gives us seven days in a week and expects us to take one day, to stop from our normal routine, to devote to Him.

We do not sin if we fail to attend church. We sin if we go about our usual work schedule, if we go to the lake without making time for God, if we watch afternoon football and fail to pause in the midst or at the end of our busy week to give God his due: one day that we consecrate or make holy to Him. That means spending time in His presence, meditating on His word, worshipping Him alone or with other followers.

He loves us. How much do we love Him? He doesn't need us, but we need Him.

V. "Honor your father and your mother."

Breaking this command also carries a death sentence. Who can say that he has never disobeyed his parents or argued with them or gotten angry at them when they have imposed discipline?

Some would argue that when they were a teenager. . . well, you know. Conflict is inevitable. That was a long time ago. Kids will be kids.

We may have forgotten such sins, but God has not. The sins of our past are just as present to God as today – with Him there is no statute of limitations. Every act of disobedience is on our record. To do something wrong that dishonors us and our family name also dishonors our parents.

God promises a long and happy life to children who honor their parents. The corollary may also be true: a short, unhappy life to those who dishonor their parents. King David's favorite son Absalom turned the people against his father. His disobedience cost Absalom his life (2 Samuel 18).

VI. *"You should not murder."*

Sometimes incorrectly translated as the more generic "Thou shall not *kill*," murder is not limited in the scriptural context to simply taking someone's life. The state executes criminals. Soldiers are killed in war. Scripture makes provision for the necessary taking of human life. But murder, with or without malice or forethought, committed in a moment of passion or in cold-blood can occur – in God's estimation, and He is the ultimate judge – not just in action, but *in thought.*

Jesus redefines the traditional understanding of murder in Matthew, chapter 5:

"You have heard it said to the people long ago, 'Do not murder and anyone who murders will be subject to

92

*judgment.' But I tell you that anyone who is **angry** with his brother will be subject to judgment."* 1 John 3:15 adds, *"Anyone who **hates** his brother without cause is a murder."*

So, unreasonable anger and hatred can be punishable by God as actual murder.

VII. "You shall not commit adultery."

The commandment against adultery is not confined to sexual infidelity by married people. The full Biblical teaching includes fornication – sex between unmarried people, and a variety of sexually impure acts: homosexuality, bestiality, incest and even lewd behavior, such as strip clubs, lap dancing or masturbation.

But again, Jesus adds to the interpretation: *"You have heard it said, 'Do not commit adultery.' But I tell you that anyone who **looks at a woman lustfully** has already committed adultery with her in his heart."*

Even looking at Playboy magazine or a pornographic website to arouse lust, sexually fantasizing about the girl in the short skirt or the guy in the tight jeans, daydreaming about a sexual encounter with some glamorous celebrity – to God this is the same as adultery.

1 Corinthians 6:9 says, *"Do not be deceived: Neither the **sexually immoral** nor **idolaters** nor **adulterers** nor **male prostitutes** nor **homosexual offenders** . . . will inherit the kingdom of heaven."*

VIII. "You shall not steal."

When asked if they have ever taken something that doesn't belong to them, most people proclaim their own goodness. Or, no, I've never robbed a bank or stolen a car.

When pressed, they might qualify their answer. Well, maybe when I was a child I took a green apple from my neighbor's tree without asking. Or, yes, I might have slipped a dollar bill out of my mother's purse. But is stealing an answer off someone's test stealing? Is cutting in line in front of someone stealing?

God goes so far as to state that if we fail to give him the first fruits of our labors, our tithes and offerings – traditionally the first ten percent of what we earn – then *we steal from God.* The earth and everything in it belongs to the Lord.

God will not allow thieves in His kingdom.

IX. *"You shall not bear false witness."*

Almost everyone who is halfway honest will admit to having lied on occasion. But again, we are like attorneys in how we excuse our dishonesty: we tell *white lies*, as if the color matters to God. Or we lie to a telemarketer we don't want to talk to. Or the usual defense is we don't want to hurt someone's feelings by being honest, so it's all right to not be brutally honest about their new haircut or weight or clothes they've asked us about.

Another experiment we conducted with 50 students was to have them correct a classmate's exam. On 70 percent of the exams students either "fudged" the correctness of an answer or they deliberately failed to count an answer wrong. If given an opportunity, a group of students once told us, every one of them would cheat if they knew they would not get caught.

To us, lying is not always lying. Sometimes it's bending the truth. Or not telling the whole truth.

Recall the famous words of Colonel Oliver North before Congress who said he did not lie, but just gave "an alternate version of the facts." But God knows the truth because He is a God of truth.

God sees our hearts and the intent of our hearts. We are told, *"All liars will have their place in the lake of fire."*

X. *"You shall not covet."*

This command is impossible to keep. Who can say he's never desired what belongs to someone else? Who has not imagined enjoying the lifestyle of the rich and famous? Who has not coveted in his heart someone else's job or fame or car or house or good looks or spouse?

By nature we want what we don't have.

We think if we stumble over one or two of these "minor" commandments – and who hasn't told a lie once or twice or coveted Bill Gate's billions? – that God will still weigh our overall goodness against a few slip-ups and let us in under the pearly gates.

The Bible says, *"For whoever keeps the whole law and yet stumbles at just one point is guilty of breaking all of it."* (James 2:10)

That may seem harsh to us, but above all, God is just: should he allow murderers into His perfect heaven? What about thieves? Or liars? He is also merciful and loving. People ask why would a loving God condemn anyone to an eternity of hell?

He does not. We condemn ourselves by what we do and fail to do. We break his moral law – the law of sin and death built into the very fabric of the universe and just as real as the law of gravity or thermodynamics. It is written on the heart (soul) of every human being.

We instinctively know right from wrong. Our conscience bears witness.

Conscience comes from the words "con" or with, and "science" or knowledge – with knowledge. Every time we break God's law, we do so *with knowledge*. He wants us to live, but our crimes against Divinity bring judgment upon us:"*The soul that sins will die*."

We also fail to accept God's loving offer – his free gift of eternal life – if we reject Jesus as our Savior and Lord.

"*He is patient with you, **not wanting anyone to perish**, but everyone to come to repentance*." (2 Peter 3:9)

What then must we do?

God created us to live in harmony with Him and with others, and to be stewards of his creation. But we rebel by breaking his moral law. Sin is lawlessness.

Approximately 20,000 murders are committed in the United States every year. Half of the murderers are never brought to justice by the legal system. Does that mean 10,000 lawbreakers got away with murder? For now, maybe. But someday each will stand before God. The evidence of their crimes will condemn them.

The evidence of our crimes – lying, stealing, lusting, coveting, disobeying parents, taking God's name in vain, failing to honor the Sabbath or put God first in our lives – will also condemn us. We are even now on death row. Our eventual death will be evidence of our guilt. And when we stand before God the judge, He will either give us justice or mercy.

Justice is what we deserve. Mercy is His love and forgiveness because Jesus Christ died on the bleak hill of Calvary outside Jerusalem 2000 years ago – for you.

. . so you would not have to be condemned to eternal death.

You can pass from death to eternal life. But—

You must come to God in this life with a humble and contrite spirit as a condemned sinner begging for mercy. If we fail to grasp the utter depravity of our souls, or if we think we can earn our way to heaven by our good works, then we deceive ourselves.

If we think we can be a Buddhist or Hindu or Muslim and not face God the Almighty for judgment, then we are wrong. Mohammed or Buddha did not die for your sins. Jesus Christ did. Allah and the Judeo-Christian God are not the same. They mutually exclude each other; to follow one you must deny the other.

Peter the apostle said of Jesus, *"Salvation is found in no one else, for there is no other name under heaven given to men by which we must be saved."*

Jesus leaves no room for any other savior. He did not come just to save the Jews or only for the Christians. He came for the whole world – every culture, tribe and race, that men and women might have forgiveness of sins and have life now and when they die.

He requires that we repent. To repent means to confess and forsake our sins. He requires that we place our faith in Him and Him alone.

Repentance and Faith – it's not rocket surgery that people cannot understand. But usually understanding is not the problem: obedience is. We want to do what we want to do. We don't want anyone telling us how to live– even God. Or we don't believe -- even with all the evidence that leads us to His love. To not believe God is to call Him a liar and thus build up His anger toward us for the eventual day of wrath.

Sinners who have not repented will be justly punished – an eternity in a lake of fire in which they will suffer torment, but never be consumed . Sinners who do repent and trust Jesus will receive forgiveness and an everlasting reward.

To say I don't believe the testimony of creation, God's revelation, the person of Jesus and the 2000 year witness of the Church is like a man atop a 100 story building who says he doesn't believe in gravity. He denies the obvious. If he jumps, he may travel halfway down and still assert, *See – I'm fine. I'm flying.* But let him fall another 50 floors and the truth of reality will become evident. His belief or disbelief does not create objective reality nor the invisible laws he will be subject to in time.

Consider the example of Dr. Anthony Flew, an eminent British philosopher and atheist. While an Oxford undergraduate in the 1940s, Flew attended the weekly meetings of C. S. Lewis's *Socratic Club.* Although he found Lewis to be "an eminently reasonable man" and "by far the most powerful of Christian apologists," for most of his life, as Flew argued in his book *The Presumption of Atheism* (1984), he or anyone else should presuppose atheism until evidence of a God surfaces.

Apparently Flew did encounter persuasive evidence of God.

In a 2004 interview article with Professor Gary Habermas entitled, *My Pilgrimage from Atheism to Theism,* Flew said, "Darwin himself, in the fourteenth chapter of *The Origin of Species,* pointed out that his whole argument began with a being which already possessed reproductive powers. This is the creature, the evolution of which, a truly comprehensive theory of evolution must give some account. Darwin himself was well aware that he had not produced such an account. It now seems to me that the findings of *more than fifty years of DNA research have provided materials for a new and enormously powerful argument to design."*

Flew said "he had to go where the evidence leads" even if that meant concluding that design implied a Master Designer, a God who created the heavens and the earth to whom we will give an account of how we have lived..

Reasonable Conclusion #7: We will not escape God's righteous judgment if we refuse His free gift of salvation through Jesus Christ?

8. How Then Should We Live?

Fact: Many who say they are Christian do not live like a Christian.

Christians are not mass-produced by a cookie cutter. They don't all go to the same church, nor read the same version of the Bible, nor wear an official "Christian" uniform or have an approved "holiness" hairstyle. Though some may adopt certain dietary principles, Jesus explicitly said, "The Kingdom of God is **not** a matter of eating and drinking but of righteousness." Paul, who wrote a third of the New Testament, made clear to Peter, a leader of the Jerusalem church, that circumcision or other rites were not the essential issue.

If we argue as a matter of dogma whether or not a Christian should attend a movie or was the "fruit of the vine" at the last supper really wine or grape juice, then we miss the crux of what it means to be a Christian.

Hindus follow a multiplicity of ascetic paths – prescriptions for right living.

Buddhists follow the noble eightfold path – prescriptions for right living.

Muslims follow the five pillars of Islam – prescriptions for right living.

Christians follow Jesus. Period.

Christians must begin at the feet of Jesus on the cross – in godly sorrow for our sinfulness. We must confess and forsake our sins – stop sinning. We must repent, which means to turn in the opposite direction, away from sin and toward God. But salvation is not what we do.

It is what Christ has already done for us. We must put our complete, total 100 percent faith in the finished work of Jesus – "*It is finished,*" he cried out at the moment of his death. He becomes our Savior (we

100

cannot save ourselves) and our Lord for the rest of this life and then into eternity.

We follow Him, the incarnate God-man who died as a flesh and blood human being, but rose again to life in a glorified body. He came to planet earth as a humble carpenter's son, born in an animal stable, unnoticed by most of the world. He lived his life as a servant. He became His Father's spotless *Lamb of God* whose mission was to take away the sin of the World.

He accomplished his mission. At this very moment he is ruling in majesty and glorious splendor in a heavenly realm we cannot even imagine. Many scholars think his return to earth – to establish his everlasting kingdom – is soon, even imminent.

How then should we live thus takes on greater meaning. We should live with the expectancy that this life is brief – just a breath – and eternity is long, and that the soon and coming king has a mission for each of us who follows him.

First, to be a Christian means to be changed by Christ. *He* changes us. He begins to reshape us from the inside out in his image to be more like him.

Second, to be a Christian means to undergo a fundamental life-change in four areas: nature, character, meaning and purpose.

We have a new nature. Every human is born with a sin nature – an inherent tendency to sin. When we are re-born or born again through repentance and faith, God transfuses us with His nature.

We can undergo a dramatic supernatural transformation through an encounter with the Living God, as did Saul, the murderous hunter of Jesus' followers who was struck blind by a blast of God's power on the road to Damascus. Or, in contrast, Paul's spiritual son Timothy was raised in a godly home and grew in spiritual strength and wisdom from a young age, but was still formed into the image of Christ, though less dramatically.

The Bible says, "If anyone is in Christ, *he is a new creation*; the old has gone, the new has come." God said in the book of Ezekiel, "I will put *my spirit in you* and move you to follow my decrees and be careful to keep my laws."

We are not just following a new path, the Christian way. **We are new.** We may not appear different in the mirror, but once we were spiritually dead in our sins (Eph 2:1-2). Our new inner self is supernaturally alive in and through Christ Jesus.

We have a new character. Character is the outward manifestation of our new internal nature, the moment by moment flow of how we live in the world.

We meet young people who have had a Christian experience at some point in their lives, who perhaps prayed a sinner's prayer, made a profession of faith, who went for a time to church or a Bible study, but then seemed to depart from the Way. What went wrong? Were they false converts who were never transformed? Were they "Christianized" – acting and talking like true believers but then abandoning their faith for some reason? Some claim to be Christians but live like pagans. What's wrong?

Many of us fail because we do not come to God on *His terms*, but ours. We want to be saved without being changed. We want forgiveness without repentance. We want God's blessing without the sufferings. We cannot be a Christian without being consecrated. If God has truly regenerated us, we should not continue to sin.

Jesus admonished some of his first century followers that not everyone who called him Lord would enter heaven, but "only those who do the *will of my Father.*"

102

What is the will of God? This is the nuts and bolts of imitating Jesus, of being conformed to him. Here are some scriptures:

*"*It is **God's will** that you should be sanctified*." (1 Thess. 4:3)

*"*Be joyful always, pray continually, give thanks in all circumstances, for this is **God's will** for you in Christ Jesus*." (1Thess. 4:16-18)

We are instructed that the mind that is in Christ should be in us – we should think like him. He is our example, the one whom we should model our life after. He fulfilled His Father's will. He was a servant. He was obedient unto death. Above all, he loved.

We should examine ourselves, to see if we are in the faith, by studying the life and character of Jesus. How do we measure up? Do we obey God's commands? Do we serve others? Are we loving? Are we sanctified (holy)?

Here's a pop quiz: which of these best describe you:

sexually immoral, impure, debauched, idolatrous, occult interests, hateful, jealous, given to rage or arguing, selfishly ambitious, envious, open to drunkenness and orgies -- or -- loving, joyful, peaceable, patient, kind, good, faithful, gentle and self-controlled?

"Those who live by the Spirit of God will not gratify the desires of the sinful nature." (Galatians 5:16)

Is our essential nature God's holy nature or the sinful nature of the flesh?

In our own strength as human beings we are not equipped to lead godly lives, no matter how much we try. The cowardly apostles hid in the upper room after Jesus' death, fearful for their lives until. . . they were **empowered** by the Holy Spirit. Then they became bold witnesses, dynamic followers, faithful martyrs.

103

If God's Holy Spirit dwells inside us, then He will strengthen our resolve to live holy, joyful, prayerful, loving lives.

To live in today's world is to be assaulted by myriad temptations: sexual images on magazine covers at the checkout; stories of lottery winners to entice even non-gamblers; telemarketers who cause even honest people to want to lie; disintegrating ethics and morality at every level.

Paul writes to the Corinthian church: *"God is faithful; he will not let you be tempted beyond what you can bear. But when you are tempted, he will also provide a way to escape, so you can bear up under it."*

We have a new meaning. What is the meaning of life? Ask a variety of people and you will get a variety of answers. For the Christian the answer is simple.

The meaning of life is that God means for us to know and love and serve Him. . . and to love and serve our fellow human beings.

That is the beginning and end of the Great Commandment. Life then is not a riddle to be solved. It is not a burden to be carried. Life is a joy to be experienced.

To view life from a purely materialistic-humanistic worldview, in which man and not God is the measure of all things is to see a human being as only matter and energy that has evolved by chance over time without any intrinsic value or meaning.

Genocide is then possible and inevitable in a world where man makes law based on no higher authority than himself and finds no meaning in life other than what he ascribes to it.

History proves how often cultural groups de-humanize those different from themselves. India's caste system considers the "untouchables," the Dalits, as less than human.

The late Dr. Francis Schaffer wrote in *The Christian Manifesto* that Our Founding Fathers created government to protect the *inalienable rights endowed by our Creator.* If given by men, such rights can be taken away by men. We have value because God created us with value. Life has meaning because God builds meaning into the essence of our being.

"*He has set eternity in the hearts of men.*" (Ecclesiastes 3:11)

Because we are created by the unfathomable mind of the Creator, shaped in His holy image, in-breathed with His Spirit, transformed by His power, imbued with His love – we have infinite value. We are not a fluke of nature. We are a handiwork of the Almighty. We are not damned to oblivion, but destined for eternity.

God said he made us "*a little below the angels.*" He adopts us as His children. We are co-heirs to inherit His kingdom and reign with Christ. We are ordained as a holy priesthood. We are appointed ambassadors.

Existentialists in the 1950s concluded if there was a God (many were atheists), then he was a) dead, b) irrelevant or c) visiting a faraway galaxy. But as much as the Communist Soviet Union or Communist China tried to eradicate Christianity, the number of Christians multiplied because in the midst of persecution, the message of the gospel provided meaning to what would otherwise seem to be a meaningless existence. God does provide answers to life's questions.

Why is there suffering and injustice in the world? Because rebellion and sin entered God's perfect creation. Someday He will restore perfection.

Why does God not intervene? In time He will, but for now He expects us, his living body of believers, to be salt and light in the world. However, how do we know He does not intervene in worldly affairs? "*In*

Him we live and breathe and have our being." He sustains all creation by His power. He "*rewards those who earnestly seek Him.*"

Why do bad things happen to good people? A study of Luke 13 (verses 1-10) reveals four reasons: 1) evil people do exist, for now; b) the world is under a curse from sin; c) we bear some responsibility for what happens; d) we have an active spiritual enemy. Many questions may not be fully answered to our satisfaction until we personally ask God in heaven. Millions of Christians can testify that a life lived in Christ has new meaning and value.

We have new purpose. Russian novelist Leo Tolstoy once asked: "What is life for? To die? To kill myself at once? No, I am afraid. To wait for death till it comes? I fear that even more. Then I must live. But what for? In order to die? I could not escape from that circle."

English political philosopher Thomas Hobbes wrote in *Leviathan* in 1651 that the life of man, "was solitary, poor, nasty, brutish, and short."

Austrian philosopher Ludwig Wittgenstein said: "I don't know why we are here, but I'm pretty sure that it is not in order to enjoy ourselves."

The narrator of the ancient book of *Ecclesiastes* surveys reasons for living – the pursuit of knowledge, wisdom, pleasures, work, success, riches – and finds them all without meaning because a common fate – death – awaits everyone. His final conclusion in the matter is this: "*Fear God and keep his commandments, for this is the whole duty of man.*"

Is that all? Is there no more profound purpose in life?

Popular bestselling author Rick Warren in *The Purpose Driven Life* has written a treatise that millions

106

of people have applied to their lives: it is that God designed us for five primary purposes:

- We were planned for God's good pleasure, so our first purpose is to offer real *worship* in prayer, praise, music, song and everything we do.
- We were formed for God's family, so our second purpose is to enjoy real *fellowship* in community with others.
- We were created to become like Christ, so our third purpose is to learn real *discipleship*, to apprentice ourselves to the Master for life
- We were shaped for serving God, so our fourth purpose is to practice real *ministry* by meeting the physical, emotional and spiritual needs of others.
- We were made for a mission, so our fifth purpose is to live out daily real *evangelism* so we share with everyone the Good News in truth and love.

How Then Should We Live?

We should live as Revolutionaries of Love. John Wesley said, "I want to live as if on fire for God so that others will come just to watch me burn."

Jesus calls us: *"If any of you wants to be my follower, you must put aside your selfish ambition, shoulder your cross, and follow me. If you try to keep your life for yourself, you will lose it. But it you give up your life for my sake and for the sake of the gospel, you will find true life."*

It's a radical call. Jesus upends the common view of how to live: the first shall be last; the greatest shall

107

be the least; we must come as little children; we must give to get; we should lay down our lives for others. He is our internal compass who points us towards the truth. He orients us in a new direction.

We are told to seek him and his kingdom of righteousness first. We are taught that all are equal in Jesus Christ: male and female, Jew and Gentile, black and white, red and yellow, rich and poor, but that we should think of and treat others **better** than ourselves. God comes first, others second, then us.

Jesus said, "*If you love me, you will* **obey** *my commands.*"

We are to be caretakers of this world, but not to love creation above the Creator. Money is not the root of all evil, but the **love** of money. Riches are to be used as a tool – to feed the hungry, clothe the naked, shelter the homeless. A rich Christian is an oxymoron, though we do build up treasure in heaven by doing good works on earth.

Consider the example of Giovanni Francesco, son of a wealthy Italian merchant.

As a young man he squandered his time. At 20 he marched off to battle to win glory in combat. But he was captured and spent a year as a prisoner. When he returned home broken in spirit and ill he examined the purpose of his life. How could he live so self-centeredly and carefree when others were suffering?

He vowed to care for the poor. His family thought him insane. As he began to treat the lepers and rebuild the abandoned churches near his home and live like a hermit, preaching to the birds, he attracted followers. A well-to-do teenage girl named Clare became a disciple of the mystical young man.

The church in Rome soon heard of and blessed the work of Francis from Assisi, then the mission of the Poor Clares.

Since the 12th Century the Franciscans have dedicated their lives of poverty, chastity and obedience in service to the world's poor.

Common sense tells us that if we honor the God who loves and saves us, that if we seek harmony and peace with others, that if we live as servants to all, we would be individually and collectively a transforming force for good. And the judge of the universe will reward us when He comes in glory.

Reasonable Conclusion #8: To live as a child of God is to live a holy life of service and love with the expectation of an eternity of unspeakable joy.

9. How Do We Walk the Talk?

*"Do not merely listen to the word, and so deceive yourselves. **Do what it says**."* (James 1:22)

Some practical advice: We are all on the same unending journey that begins at conception and continues beyond this life. Wisdom books tell us we are exiles in this world, sojourners passing through – that we should travel light and live simply.

Most of humanity lives in poverty of one sort or another: material, moral, spiritual. Only in Him do we find freedom. *El Shaddi* – the Almighty God – wishes for no one to perish, but all to come to repentance. He is ultimate reality, and by His will everything that exists was created and has its being. We live because He lives in us.

Salvation is a gift many refuse. But once we answer His call and accept His outstretched love, He has a way of re-ordering our priorities. Like a potter, He shapes the soft clay of our lives into sacred vessels. Like a master jeweler He grinds away rough edges and cleanses us of dross. We live as a work in progress.

We live moment by moment in the presence of God, but our awareness fluctuates. Because He is real, He is engaged in all we are and are becoming. **Prayer** should be the heartbeat of our life in Him. As a loving Father, He longs that we spend time in His presence, that we develop trust and intimacy. If we rarely conversed with our earthly father, what kind of relationship would that be? Our Heavenly Father is never more than a thought away. If we wait until Sundays and then only repeat a formalized prayer, we develop only a superficial, impersonal relationship.

Our soul longs to swim in the sea of His unfathomable love, to be replenished, to let Him speak

110

to us in deep silence. Prayer is communion, a holy encounter because He is holy.

He has given us a primary care manual for our soul in His word, the **Bible**. For most Christians it remains a closed book. We should read it thoughtfully, prayerfully and systematically. It nourishes our inner selves.

*"Man does not live by bread alone, but by **every word** that comes from the mouth of God."*

Do we eat food for our body every day? What if we ate only once a week? We would not be too healthy. We need spiritual food every day as well. God's word is living and active – it feeds our soul. If we spend a total of 1-2 hours daily eating earthly food, we should spend at least as much time ingesting His spiritual food.

God's Holy Spirit will help us understand the scriptures. An unbeliever will read only words in a book that seem dense and dull -- myths, fables and moralizing. However, when our spirit is energized by His Spirit, it is as if a light is switched on in our consciousness. We will crave the meat of God's word. It will come alive. We will cross over from this world of shadows into a realm of timelessness.

We should read it *literarily*, understanding how each, individual book flows into the whole narrative from Creation to the establishment of His never-ending kingdom.

The Bible is not a novel; it is history, poetry, prophecy, documentary, legal teaching – each literary genre requires our understanding. We should read the text in *context* and interpret it literally when the context requires us to do so. Jesus' command to "Feed the poor," is intended to be understood literally. But when he says, "I am the bread of life," the context implies a figurative or metaphorical meaning. Memorize his word; it is a wellspring of life.

Church is not a building. It is believers, the followers of Jesus who gather in community.

It is also a verb, the active, ongoing ministry work of God on earth through those who are called to serve as faithful laborers. Everyone who names the name of the Lord is a worker in His vineyard. We are brothers and sisters in Christ's Body. We have an intimate, family bond with every other believer throughout history and around the world. God's love becomes the universal language.

Some criticize the church for its lack of unity. Why so many denominations? But the variety of churches should be seen as a vibrant sign of health. Christians are not programmed as robots.

Every cultural group brings its uniqueness to the body of Christ, and within countries like the United States, diversity in style or approach strengthens the church. Southern African-American Full Gospel churches are distinctly different from traditional New England Protestant or Catholic churches – but in core beliefs and fundamentals of the faith – agreement embraces diversity.

We should live **holy lives**, avoiding sin, even the appearance of sin. Most Christians fail to understand what living a holy life requires. Simply put, we should stop sinning. We should not lie. We should not steal. We should not covet or use God's name in vain. The 10 Commandments are God's universal standard, written in stone. If we continue to sin – even when we try not to – perhaps we have not truly repented (U-turn) and surrendered our body/soul/spirit to God? If we belong to Him and are His servants, we cannot also be slaves to sin. We cannot serve two masters.

To sin is to make a conscious, willful decision to disobey God. Sin is an act of *our* will. We must *will* to rebel. If someone insults us, *we decide* (will) to respond

112

in anger or in love. We cannot blame God for our failings. Nor should we blame Satan. He is a formidable adversary who does have an insurgent army, but as a Christian we have weapons in our arsenal for the spiritual battle.

"If we confess our sins, He is faithful and just to forgive us our sins and cleanse us from all unrighteousness." (1 John 1:9)

Some apply this scripture as a casual attitude to their own sin -- a ready antidote when they stumble and fall. Some go so far as to give themselves liberty to sin because "God will always forgive my sins." Just as 007 James Bond had a "license" to kill, we have James 1/1:9 as a license to sin.

But such a *laissez faire* approach is poor justification to sin with abandon. Sin causes corruption. It is a cancer that eats away our soul.

Every sin is a sin against God. Every sin tramples underfoot the ultimate act of love – Jesus' death for us. Every sin grieves God.

We have had students say *we cannot stop sinning.* The pressure from peers is too great. The power of sin is too strong. Long-time, ingrained habits are too hard to break. Sin has too great a hold on our minds, wills and emotions. We have surrendered parts of our bodies – our eyes, our mouth, our sexual organs to the enemy – and he refuses to give them back.

God's servant Job in chapter 31 said: "*I made a* **covenant** *with my eyes to not look lustfully at a girl.*" A covenant is a sacred promise, a contract written in blood. We can do the same to avoid lust of the eyes.

Isaiah cried out in 6:5, "*I am a man of unclean lips.*" But God touched his lips with a burning coal from the heavenly altar and purified his speech. We can surrender our tongues to God and not to the devil.

Blessings and curses should not flow out from the same cistern.

We should offer ourselves as "*a living sacrifice, holy,* and acceptable to God, which is our reasonable service," – reasonable because He expects us to live holy lives. He would not require us to do what is impossible without giving us the ability to obey. If we consecrate ourselves to Him, *He will make us righteous.* When *we* try to do His work the result is *self-righteous.* To approach the Living God in our unholy state would be suicide -- His consuming fire of Holiness would devour us.

If we had a clear vision of God for only ten seconds, or the reality of hell and its souls in torment, or the blinding glory of heaven, we could not continue to live half-asleep, wrapped in our self-complacency. We have no excuse for sin.

"*Without holiness, no one will see the Lord.*" (Hebrews 12:14)

Spread the word is our commission – not just for those in silk robes or evangelist suits and ties. Good News *is* truly good news for every creature.

Imagine driving along a rain-slick road after a thunderstorm. You skid and fishtail and come to a stop at the edge of a cliff where a swollen river has washed away the bridge. Inches farther and you would have plunged off a thousand foot precipice.

Do you turn around and drive away? Or do you feel compelled to warn other drivers. In fact, at that instant a speeding motorist drives by you and off into space. You see the headlights of others approaching. Some are friends, your family. You are safe. But do you feel any responsibility to those who don't know what lies ahead?

Everyone you know is headed for the cliffs of eternity.

114

Will you let them perish? Or will you jump into their path and scream and wave your arms to get their attention before it's too late?

People perish forever if they die without the Savior's mercy. If we know the truth and do not warn people, we will be held responsible for their fate.

Welcome to the war. We step out from the kingdom of darkness and powers of sin and death at the moment of new birth and become changed in our inner beings to children of light.

Despite what happy-talk preachers might say, living daily as a Christian is not magically easier. We are to cinch up our belts and live alert and vigilant. Expect attack. When you go over to the other side, an army of demon spirits marks you as a traitor. But you now have angelic protection and the most powerful force in all the cosmos dwells inside you.

But to not know your enemy or how to wield the battle weapons you have available is to live in ignorance. Knowledge is power. Power is victory.

Jesus promises us an abundant life, but not a life free of struggle. Throughout history His followers have been persecuted. But He will "*never leave or forsake*" us. The journey may be tempestuous, but we will arrive safely at our destination.

A consuming passion should draw us closer to the Living God. If He is not our first thought in the morning, our last at night and a continual, vital presence throughout our day then we need a self-check.

In the parable of the sower (Matthew 13), Jesus warns of those who receive the seeds of good news but then fail along the way. In fact, 3 out of 4 die out – that's a 75 percent crop failure. Of those who do produce a crop, some yield 30 times more, some 60, some a bumper crop of 100 plus – but only from the ¼ firmly planted in good soil.

115

Are we growing? Stagnating? Are we Christian in name only?

When God enters our names into the Lamb's Book of Life, He invites us as co-authors to help write today's chapter of universal history. The pages of the future have yet to be completed. What will we add?

Each new day is a gift to us from the Giver of Life. How then shall we live?

Reasonable Conclusion #9 – Today is the acceptable day of salvation.

10. Roll Call of Faith

American media mogul Ted Turner once said, "Christianity is for losers," which echoes French author Voltaire's famous quote: "Christianity is the most ridiculous, the most absurd, and bloody religion that has ever infected the world."

Former Minnesota Governor and professional wrestler Jesse Ventura, in paraphrasing Karl Marx, chimed in: "Organized religion is a sham and a crutch for weak-minded people who need strength in numbers."

German philosopher Friedrich Nietzsche, who declared "God is dead," and who spent his final years of life in a mental asylum, also said, "In Christianity neither morality nor religion come into contact with reality at any point."

Edgar Allan Poe, inventor of the modern gothic tale wrote, "All religion is simply evolved out of chicanery, fear, greed, imagination and poetry."

And psychoanalyst Sigmund Freud: "Religion is an illusion and it derives its strength from its readiness to fit in with our instinctual wishful impulses."

These well-known figures are entitled to their opinions, but the historical record proves otherwise: many of the greatest political leaders, scientists, philosophers, artists, writers and musicians have not hidden the fact they were followers of Jesus Christ.

Here is only a brief listing of 100 who significantly impacted the world – and who were Christians.

Charlemagne (742-814)

Latin for "Charles the Great," Charlemagne was the son of Pepin III, King of the Franks, named after his grandfather, Charles Martel, who had stopped the

Saracens from overrunning Gaul (modern France) ten years before he was born.

He succeeded his father in 768 as ruler over the tribes of Western Europe. At nearly 6-feet-four inches he was a commanding figure, leading his army to defeat the Saxons, the Lombards, the Slavs, the Avars -- extending his reign across all of central Europe to the Adriatic and Byzantine Empire. His clash with the Spanish Moors in the Pyrenees Mountains inspired the epic poem, *The Song of Roland.*

At St. Peter's basilica on Christmas Day, A.D. 800, Pope Leo III placed a golden crown on his head and proclaimed Charles Emperor of the Holy Roman Empire with the words, "Behold another Constantine, who has risen in our times."

Charlemagne was deeply pious, often attending church four times a day. He regarded himself as the divinely appointed Defender of the Faith. "Our task is, with God's help, to defend with our arms the holy Church of Christ against attacks by the heathen from any side . . . so that the name of our Lord Jesus Christ may be glorified throughout the world."

The book, *City of God,* by 5th century church father Augustine, which sets forth ideals on how to govern a temporal kingdom influenced Charlemagne's rule. He undertook needed reforms in the church; he combated heresies; missionaries traveled with his armies; he directed a revision of the Bible, and he required monasteries and churches to open schools to educate the poor,

Dante Alighieri (1265-1321)

Dante's poetic journey through Hell and Purgatory to Paradise -- *The Divine Comedy* -- is one of the great spiritual works of Western Literature. City-states vied for power in Italy during Dante's lifetime and the political turbulence of Florence resulted in Dante's exile from his beloved home for the last twenty years of his life.

But in exile he was able to complete his masterwork, composed of 100 cantos (between 130 and 150 verses each) in three glorious canticles of *terza rima*, a form in which the first and third lines rhyme, while the middle line rhymes with the subsequent stanza.

Traditionally, a "comedy" is a story that begins "in sorrow and ends in joy." The purpose of Dante's *Commedia* was to convert a corrupt society to righteousness, "to remove those living in this life from a state of misery and lead them to a state of felicity."

For Dante, the Creator's handiwork was everywhere evident: "Nature is the art of God."

"Heaven wheels above you, displaying to you her eternal glories, and still your eyes are on the ground"

At the end of his journey, in book three, Dante soars beyond the planets, beyond the stars, and beholds the whole company of Heaven assembled together, and is given a vision of the glory of God Himself -- the unimaginable boundless space that "has no 'where' but in the mind of God."

William Butler Yeats called him "the chief imagination of Christendom," and T. S. Eliot said: "Dante and Shakespeare divide the modern world between them. There is no third."

Nicholas Copernicus (1473-1543)

Copernicus was the Polish astronomer who formulated the first mathematically based system of planets going around the sun. His research contradicted long-held beliefs that the earth was center of our solar system.

After his studies at the University of Cracow, he received a doctorate in canon law in Italy, then he trained in medicine – a skill he would use as a physician to the poor of Frauenburg, Poland where he was a clerical advisor to the cathedral. His great interest, however, was astronomy, and he turned his tower apartment into a night observatory using homemade instruments, "to seek the truth in all things, in so far as God has granted that to human reason" – even if that meant challenging centuries of scientific dogma.

Reluctant to publish, shortly after his book appeared, *On the Revolutions of Heavenly Bodies* in 1543, he became ill and died. Despite solid reasoning, his contemporaries could not accept his conclusions that the earth rotated on its axis once daily and traveled around the sun once yearly: a fantastic concept – until Galileo confirmed Copernicus' assertions a century later.

A brilliant scientist, diplomat, linguist, artist and humble Christian who saw no theological conflict in his work, Copernicus concluded, "My goal is to find the truth in God's majestic creation."

Michelangelo (1475-1564)

The Italian Renaissance titan who excelled as a sculptor, painter, architect and poet created on the Sistine Chapel ceiling in Rome the world's greatest religious masterpiece -- over a space half the size of a football field – by himself, painting on his back for four years, 70 feet above the concrete floor. A marvel of draftsmanship, vibrant color and fresco technique, the ceiling depicts the vast creation cycle of Genesis up to the Flood with parallel episodes of Moses, the lawgiver, and Christ, the savior.

Over 343 larger than life-sized figures across nine central panels display Michelangelo's genius and his quest to discover God through his art as others seek God in prayer.

"The true work of art is but a shadow of the divine perfection."

Alternating his home between Florence with Medici patronage and Rome where a succession of popes employed Michelangelo's talents, he created some of the most profound art the world has known: the *Pietas* and *David* sculptures; *Conversion of St. Paul* and *Martyrdom of St. Peter* frescoes on the Pauline Chapel; the *Crucifixion* drawings and *Last Judgment* painting – all, as he testified, so that God would reveal Himself through his Art.

In his poetry he was even more explicit: "Oh flesh, oh blood, oh cross, oh suffering in extremis, grant that my sins be justified in your eyes."

"Only your blood, Lord, can wash me and cleanse me of my sins."

"You alone are the seed of pure and pious works."

Michelangelo reveals in his letters that his creative concern was for the glory of God, and his Art was a means to serve the Creator who flowed so powerfully through his servant's work. "Solely for the love of God," he wrote.

Sir Francis Bacon (1561-1626)

The youngest son of the Lord Keeper of the Great Seal of England, Bacon, born in London, was a philosopher best known for establishing the scientific method based on experimentation and inductive reasoning. In *The Advancement of Learning* (1605)

121

Bacon proposed a master plan of education and in *New Atlantis* (1627) envisioned a utopian community of scholars engaged in collecting and analyzing data of every field.

"But anyone who properly considers the subject, will find natural philosophy to be, after the word of God, the surest remedy against superstition, and the most approved support of faith. She is therefore rightly bestowed upon religion as a most faithful attendant, for the one exhibits the will and the other the power of God."

Eventually promoted to Lord Chancellor of England under James I in 1618, Bacon died as the result of a scientific experiment: he became ill from stuffing a chicken with snow to test if cold would slow decay. His impact upon the quest for truth eventually led to the creation of the Royal Society for the Advancement of Science in 1662.

"For beyond all doubt there is a single and summary law in which nature centres and which is subject and subordinate to God."

William Shakespeare (1564-1616)

The greatest writer of the English language – poet, dramatist, actor – a man for all seasons and all time who probed the depths of the human heart was, in the estimation of modern critics, purely a humanist who never declared any faith in any God.

Not true. We have the historical record of his Last Will and Testament finalized in January, 1616 and signed by five witnesses in March, a month before he died. Because his death was unexpected, we have no evidence to suggest that anyone put words into his mouth.

The text reads: "*In the name of God, Amen. I, William Shakespeare of Stratford-upon-Avon in the county of Warwick, gent., in perfect health and memory, God be praised, do make and ordain this my last will and testament in manner and form following. That is to say, first, I commend my soul into the hands of God my Creator, hoping and assuredly believing, through the only merits of Jesus Christ my Saviour, to be made partaker of life everlasting, and my body to the earth whereof it is made.*"

Moreover, the entire canon of Shakespeare's 38 plays, 154 sonnets, miscellaneous poems and writings is filled with Biblical references. The last fifteen years of his life coincided with the monumental, authorized translation of the Bible under the then English monarch, King James, who was patron to Shakespeare's acting company under the title, The King's Majesty's Servants. Shakespeare intimately knew the scriptures.

He had received a sound Classical education at the Stratford Grammar School where he would have studied Greek and Roman writers, Latin, the Geneva Bible (1576) and read aloud from the English Book of Common Prayer.

One literary scholar, Naseeb Shaheen, in *Biblical References in Shakespeare's Plays,* has found over 1000 references to the Christian scriptures from every book of the Bible except Habakkuk in the Old Testament and the two short letters of John in the New. By examining the historical and literary sources of Shakespeare's plays, Shaeen makes a convincing case for Shakespeare's deep familiarity with the scriptures. For example:

In *Hamlet*, 1.2.244: "Though hell itself should gape." In *Isaiah* 5.14: "*Therefore gapeth hell.*"

123

In *Henry V*, 4.1.80: "And dying so, death is to him advantage." In *Philippians* 1.21: *"For Christ is to me life, and death is to me advantage."*

In *As You Like It*, 3.2.116; "The tree yields bad fruit." In *Matthew* 7:18: "A good tree cannot bring forth bad fruit."

Over 1000 Bible references can be found in Shakespeare. The book of Psalms provides 120 references in the bard's plays, and hundreds more reference the Book of Common Prayer, all of which make a compelling case.

Shakespeare and Miguel Cervantes, one of the greatest writers of the Spanish language and originator of the modern novel, *Don Quixote*, died on the same day, April 23, 1616. Cervantes once said: "Among the attributes of God, although they are all equal, mercy shines with even more brilliancy than justice."

Galileo Galilei (1564-1642)

Born in Pisa, Italy the eldest of seven children and considered the greatest scientific intellect of the Renaissance, Galileo is often remembered for his conflict with the Roman Catholic Church. When his controversial *Dialogue Concerning the Two Chief World Systems -- Ptolemaic & Copernican* was published in 1632, he was tried and found guilty of heresy – principally for supporting the Copernican model, though his work offered no support for a sun-centered system, his telescope discoveries did not indicate a moving earth, and his one "proof" based upon the tides was invalid. He even ignored the correct elliptical orbits of planets published twenty-five years earlier by Kepler.

In defense he stated, "I do not feel obliged to believe that the same God who has endowed us with

124

sense, reason, and intellect has intended us to forgo their use."

He had, however, offended his old friend, now Pope Urban VIII who thought Galileo had deceived him into sanctioning a view in contradiction to Church dogma. After the "trial," Galileo was exiled to his villa near Florence and forbidden to teach the sun-centered system. He did complete his most significant work in physics (1636) on the properties of solid bodies, accelerated motion and dynamics.

Until his death, Galileo expressly contended that the Bible cannot err, and saw his system as an alternate interpretation of the biblical texts. Though today some would contend that the Galileo controversy proves Science should trump Scripture, Galileo stated, "The Book of Nature is written in mathematics," as being rationally understood and a compliment to scripture. "God is known by nature in his works and by doctrine in his revealed word."

Ironically, the traditional beliefs Galileo opposed ultimately belonged to Aristotle and not to Biblical exegesis. Pseudo-scientific philosophy had become interwoven with traditional Catholic teachings during the time of Augustine in the 5th Century. Therefore, the Church's dogmatic defense of *tradition* was the controversy, not the Bible.

In fact, Psalm 19:6 says of the sun, "his going forth is from the end of the heaven, and his circuit unto the ends of it" – a description of the sun's movement science scoffed at for centuries. Modern discoveries do prove that the sun travels through space at about 600,000 miles per hour on a heavenly orbit it completes once every 200 million years.

Johannes Kepler (1571-1630)

Kepler was a brilliant German mathematician and astronomer whose early work on light confirmed the laws of planetary motion and advanced Copernicus' heliocentric theory. He also came close to reaching the Newtonian concept of universal gravity – half a century before Newton was born.

A pious Lutheran, whose works on astronomy contain writings about how space and the heavenly bodies represent the Trinity of God, Kepler suffered no persecution for his open avowal of the sun-centered system, and was allowed as a Protestant to stay in Catholic Graz as a Professor (1595-1600) when other Protestants had been expelled.

Invited by the great Danish astronomer Tycho Brahe, also a devout Christian, to collaborate on planetary observations in Prague, Kepler succeeded Brahe in 1601 – at age 30 – as Imperial Mathematician, a position he held for the rest of his life.

"Since we astronomers are priests of the highest God in regard to the book of nature, it befits us to be thoughtful, not of the glory of our minds, but rather, above all else, of the glory of God."

Rene Descartes (1596-1650)

Descartes was a French mathematician, scientist and philosopher who has been called the father of modern philosophy. His studies at a Jesuit school left him dissatisfied with previous philosophy: he had a deep religious faith as a Roman Catholic, which he kept to his dying day, along with a resolute desire to systematize all knowledge.

Inspired by a dream in 1619, Descartes began to formulate his life's work: developing a proper method for engaging science and rational theology. His

126

famous quote: *I think, therefore I am*, is actually only a partial quote. His quote from the Latin is: *Dubito ergo cogito; cogito ergo sum* – I doubt, therefore I think; I think therefore I am.

Thus, while skepticism is often a necessary first step to acquiring true knowledge, history has forgotten Descartes' next step was to establish the near certainty of the existence of God - for only if God both exists and would not want us to be deceived by our experiences - can we trust our senses and logical thought processes. Therefore, God is central to his whole philosophy.

Though we may sometimes fall into error in our reasoning, he suggested, we will not do so if we accept only those truths that we *clearly and distinctly perceive*. For our rational faculties are, he claimed, given to us by God, and God is no deceiver. He thus made knowledge of the existence of God the foundation of all empirical knowledge.

"It is quite evident that existence can no more be separated from the essence of God than the fact that its three angles equal two right angles can be separated from the essence of a triangle." *Meditations on First Philosophy, Fifth Meditation*

In his *Third Mediation* Descartes says, "By the name God I understand a substance that is infinite, independent, all-knowing, all-powerful, and by which I myself and everything else, if anything else does exist, has been created."

Blaise Pascal (1623-1662)

A precocious French physicist and mathematician, at age 16 Pascal wrote *Treatise on Conic Sections* (Pascal's Theorem), and by 20 he invented a mechanical calculator, the first of its kind. At age 21 he read the work of Galileo's pupil Torricelli on the barometer, then devoted the next seven years to experiments with liquids and gasses, resulting in what today is known as Pascal's Principle. By applying it, he invented the modern syringe and the hydraulic press.

When he was 31, less than eight years before his death, Pascal experienced the overwhelming presence of God on the evening of November 23, 1654. He apparently made hasty notes that he transcribed onto a piece of parchment found sewn into the lining of his coat after his death. Illuminated by the word FEU (fire), which opens the mystical text, there is no evidence of his having mentioned the experience to anyone while he lived. From the event he wrote this prayer:

"Almighty God, who gave your servant Blaise Pascal a great intellect, that he might explore the mysteries of your creation, and who kindled in his heart a love for you and a devotion to your service: Mercifully give us your servants, according to our various callings, gifts of excellence in body, mind, and will, and the grace to use them diligently and to your glory, through Jesus Christ our Lord, who lives and reigns with you and the Holy Spirit, one God, now and forever."

In his final years he devised a modern omnibus system for Paris, for which he obtained a patent, and he began his masterwork, a defense of Christianity which he never completed but which was published after his death as *Thoughts on Religion*.

"There is a God-shaped vacuum in the heart of every man which cannot be filled by any created thing, but only by God, the Creator, made known through Jesus Christ."

"But by Jesus Christ and in Jesus Christ, we prove God and teach doctrine and morals. Jesus Christ, then, is the true God of men."

Robert Boyle (1627-1691)

Born the 14th child of the first Earl of Cork in Ireland, Boyle is often called the father of modern chemistry. He is best known for giving his name to "Boyle's Law" for the behavior of gas pressure to volume. He was a founder of the Royal Society of London who also studied respiration, blood circulation, sound, color and electricity.

As a devout Protestant, Boyle took a special interest in promoting Christianity abroad, giving money to translate and publish the New Testament into Irish and Turkish, and donating generously to missions in India. In 1690 he developed his theological views in *The Christian Virtuoso*, which he wrote to show that the study of nature was a central religious duty.

"God may rationally be supposed to have framed so great and admirable an automaton as the world for special ends and purposes."

Sir Isaac Newton (1642-1727)

Born on Christmas Day in the year Galileo died, Isaac Newton was an undisputed genius and innovator in astronomy, mechanics, and mathematics. He developed modern calculus on a single, rural sojourn in 1665-66, along with many basic laws of optics, the three laws of motion and of gravitation. In all his science, including chemistry, he saw mathematics and numbers as central.

What is less well known is that he was devoutly religious and saw numbers as involved in understanding God's plan of creation. In his system of physics, God is essential to the nature and absoluteness of space. In *Principia* he stated,

"All variety of created objects which represent order and life in the universe could happen only by the willful reasoning of its original Creator, Whom I call the Lord God."

After his studies at Cambridge University in 1665, Newton began to fill notebooks with his observations – including the fall of an apple in an orchard which led to calculations on gravitational forces. He experimented with prisms to study light and optics, which led him to build the first refracting telescope. Though the telescope was only six inches long, he concluded from his observations that the solar system itself could not have been produced by blind chance but only by a Being, "very well skilled in mechanics and geometry."

When Newton's work first appeared, it was regarded as incontrovertible evidence of a design in the universe, pointing to a Creator God. At the end of the *Principia*, Newton writes, "The most beautiful system of the Sun, Planets and Comets could only proceed from the counsel and dominion of an intelligent and powerful being, a God in fact."

In addition to his books on science, Newton left voluminous writings on theology, chronology and chemistry. When he died, he was the first scientist honored with burial in Westminster Abbey.

George Frideric Handel (1685-1759)

Born in Saxony, Germany, Handel spent most of his professional life as a composer of operas in England. His crowning work, the ***Messiah***, with its thundering "Hallelujah Chorus," an oratorio or "sacred opera," for voices set to texts from the Bible was first performed at a charity concert in 1742 in Dublin, Ireland.

Facing debt and failing health when Handel undertook to write the Messiah, he locked himself into his workroom and rarely left, even to take his meals. After 24 nonstop days he had completed 260 manuscript pages that most music critics claim come as close to pure inspiration as any music before or since.

He was said to have remarked after the intense days of composition that "I did think I did see all Heaven before me, and the great God Himself."

The first performance raised 400 pounds and freed 142 men from debtor's prison, a fate Handel himself often worried about. But with the popular success of Messiah, his fortunes increased again. Many of his subsequent concerts were benefits for the Foundling Hospital to care for orphans, of which Handel was a major benefactor.

Throughout his life Handel exhibited a deep sense of spirituality. He would often declare the pleasure he felt in setting the Scriptures to music.

In a letter to his brother-in-law written at Handel's mother's death, he said, "It pleased the Almighty, to whose great Holy Will I submit myself with Christian submission."

As his health declined in the spring of 1759 he expressed his desire to die on Good Friday, "in hopes of meeting his good God, his sweet Lord and Savior, on the day of his Resurrection." He died the day before Easter.

Handel was buried in Westminster Abbey with 3,000 in attendance. A statue at the site shows him holding a page from Messiah, the opening section of Part Three – "I know that my Redeemer lives."

Johann Sebastian Bach (1685-1750)

The father of an eminent musical dynasty of Baroque composers and performers, Johann Sebastian was born into a family of ardent Christians.

Orphaned at nine, he was raised by an older brother, himself an organist. Known to tramp miles across the idyllic German countryside to attend a music concert as a boy, the future great organist and composer of sacred and secular work, Bach once walked to the Cathedral at Lubeck – a 200 mile trek. After being so moved by the joyous music he heard, he announced his life's purpose: to create "church music to the glory of God."

At 17 Bach was appointed to his first position as the church organist in Arnstadt, but over time he would win acclaim throughout Europe for his masterworks for voice and instruments. His creative imagination produced an immense variety of musical forms that fill 60 volumes of scores.

Four of his sons revealed outstanding musical gifts, as well: Wilhelm, Carl Philipp Emanuel, Johann Christoph and Johann Christian, the youngest, who played a decisive influence on the work of another prodigy – the then nine-year old Mozart.

Among Bach's best known works are: the Brandenburg concertos, Mass in B Minor, the St. Matthew and St. John Passions, the Christmas Oratorio, the Magnificat and The Art of the Fugue. He routinely initialed his manuscripts with the letters S.D.G. – "*Soli Deo Gloria*" -- To God alone the glory.

"Where there is devotional music, God is always at hand with His gracious presence."

Franz Joseph Haydn (1732-1809)

Leading composer of the Classical Period, Father of the Symphony, the Sonata and the String Quartet,

Haydn was a life-long resident of Austria who spent most of his life as a *kapellmeister* or court musician to the wealthy Eszterházy family.

Working under the patronage of Prince Paul, Haydn produced an amazing 104 symphonies, 76 string quartets, masses, oratorios, operas, concerti, and chamber works.

As a devout Catholic, Haydn often turned to his rosary when he had trouble composing, a practice that he usually found to be effective. When he began and finished a composition, he would write *"In Nomini Jesu"* – In the Name of Jesus, and "*Laus Deo*" --Praise Be to God – on the manuscript. He also awakened early and prayed on his knees daily before beginning to compose.

Haydn once wrote about struggling to create a certain sacred work: "I prayed to God – not like a miserable sinner in despair – but calmly, slowly. In this I felt that an infinite God would surely have mercy on his finite creature, pardoning dust for being dust."

One of his greatest works, The Creation (1798) was written to inspire "the adoration and worship of the Creator," and to put the listener "in a frame of mind where he is more susceptible to the kindness and omnipotence of the Creator."

He always claimed his musical talents were an unmerited gift from God. "I offer all my praises to Almighty God, for I owe them to Him alone."

When he died in 1809 he was considered the greatest composer of his day. Even Napoleon, whose French troops had recently occupied Vienna, out of respect for Haydn sent an honor guard to escort the funeral procession.

Wolfgang Amadeus Mozart (1756-1791)

Amadeus – loved by God. Even at age three and obvious to everyone around him was the musical genius of the child prodigy who once said, "God is ever before my eyes. I realize His omnipotence and I fear His anger' but I also recognize His love, His compassion, and His tenderness towards His creatures."

By age five he was composing minuets, touring Europe at six, able to play a violin concerto or accompany a symphony on a harpsichord while grown musicians could only stand and marvel.

Modern film depictions of Mozart have distorted the real historical person as profane and a libertine. In fact, Mozart was a devoted husband to his wife Constanze, a loving father to his two children, but above all committed to his music as to honor God. He wrote, "Let come what will, nothing can go ill as it is the will of God; and that it may so go is my daily prayer."

Mozart composed masterpieces in every genre in which he wrote, and his spirituality is evident in some of his greatest compositions: Ave Verum Corpus; in 41 symphonies, notably, 40 in G minor and No. 41 in C major, the Jupiter; and his last great work, the Requiem which he left unfinished on his deathbed at age 35.

He wrote in a letter before he died, "Let us put our trust in God and console ourselves with the thought that all is well, if it is in accordance with the will of the Almighty, as He knows best what is profitable and beneficial to our temporal happiness and our eternal salvation."

Napoleon Bonaparte (1769-1821)

General of the French Revolution and Emperor of France, who once said, "I have been called to change the world," he is also remembered for establishment of the Napoleonic Code. His campaigns are studied at military academies all over the world and he is regarded as one of the greatest commanders to have ever lived.

He expressed the following thoughts while he was exiled on the rock of St. Helena. There, the conqueror of civilized Europe had time to reflect on his accomplishments. He called his longtime adjutant, Count Montholon, to his side and asked him, "Can you tell me who Jesus Christ was?" The count did not respond, so Napoleon said:

"Well then, I will tell you. Alexander, Caesar, Charlemagne and I myself have founded great empires; but upon what did these creations of our genius depend? Upon force. Jesus alone founded His empire upon love, and to this very day millions will die for Him. . .

"I think I understand something of human nature; and I tell you, all these were men, and I am a man; none else is like Him: Jesus Christ was more than a man. . .

"All who sincerely believe in Him, experience that remarkable, supernatural love toward Him. This phenomenon is unaccountable; it is altogether beyond the scope of man's creative powers. Time, the great destroyer, is powerless to extinguish this sacred flame; time can neither exhaust its strength nor put a limit to its range. This is it, which strikes me most; I have often thought of it.

"This it is which proves to me quite convincingly the Divinity of Jesus Christ."

On another occasion he said, "The nature of Christ's existence is mysterious, I admit; but this mystery meets the wants of man. Reject it and the world is an inexplicable riddle; believe it, and the history of our race is satisfactorily explained."

135

And in speaking of the Christian scriptures: "The Bible is no mere book, but a Living Creature, with a power that conquers all that oppose it."

Ludwig Van Beethoven (1770-1827)

Considered the greatest composer who ever lived, Beethoven battled increasing deafness for the last 30 years of his life. Nevertheless, neither his creative drive nor his Christian faith ever wavered. "In whatsoever manner it be, let me turn to Thee and become fruitful in good works."

The author of such profound Christian masterpieces as Mass in C, Missa Solemnis, his oratorio "Christ on the Mount of Olives," Pastoral and the Ninth Symphony, with its resounding "Ode to Joy," the German composer declared, "I will submit myself to all inconsistency and will place all my confidence in your eternal goodness, O God! My soul shall rejoice in Thee, immutable Being. Be my rock, my light, forever my trust!"

To a friend in 1810 he wrote, "I know, however, that God is nearer to me than others. I go without fear to Him. I have constantly recognized and understood Him." And to his former piano student and patron, Austrian Archduke Rudolph, Beethoven wrote, "Nothing higher exists than to approach God more than other people and from that to extend his glory among humanity."

Although Beethoven withdrew more into himself as his hearing diminished, he confessed in his *Heiligenstadt* Testament, "Almighty God, you look down into my innermost soul, you see into my heart and you know that it is filled with love for humanity and a desire to do good."

When he fell ill of pneumonia and complications in Vienna he assured his brother he was ready to make peace with his Creator: "God is with me!" He took communion and died as a thunder storm raged outside. Despite a life of unimaginable difficulties, by sheer will and faith in the God who had endowed him with musical genius as a sacred trust, Beethoven left the world a musical legacy unrivaled today.

Michael Faraday (1791-1867)

Born poor and largely self-educated, Faraday was the son of a blacksmith who became one of the greatest scientists and chemists of the 19th century. Considered the world's greatest experimental physicist, his work on electricity and magnetism revolutionized physics and laid the scientific groundwork for today's computers and telephone lines.

He was the discoverer of benzene, electromagnetic induction and the laws of electrochemistry. He was the first to convert mechanical energy into electric energy, the crucial step towards development of the electric motor and generator. Faraday developed some of the vocabulary still used in physics today, such terms as electrode, cathode, and electrolysis.

Faraday wrote that a Christian finds his guide to life in the word of God, and commits the keeping of his soul into the hands of God. "Since peace is alone in the gift of God; and since it is He who gives it, why should we be afraid? His unspeakable gift in His beloved Son is the ground of no doubtful hope."

In a sermon he delivered in London in 1861 Faraday said, "And therefore, brethren, we ought to value the privilege of knowing God's truth far beyond anything we can have in this world. The more we see the perfection of God's law fulfilled in Christ, the more we ought to thank God for His unspeakable gift."

Sojourner Truth (1797-1883)

The abolitionist and women's rights activist known for her powerful speech "Ain't I A Woman?" was born Isabella Baumfree, herself a slave in southeastern New York. Forced to submit to the will of her third master, John Dumont, Isabella married an older slave named Thomas. Thomas and Isabella had five children. She stayed on the Dumont farm until a few months before the state of New York ended slavery in 1828.

In her autobiography she said, "God revealed himself, with all the suddenness of a flash of lightning, showing her, 'in the twinkling of an eye, that he was all over,' that he pervaded the universe, 'and that there was no place where God was not."

God also gave her a new name – Sojourner, "because I was to travel up an' down the land, showin' the people their sins, an bein' a sign unto them." God then gave her a second name: "the Lord gave me Truth, because I was to declare the truth to the people."

She met the popular author of *Uncle Tom's Cabin*, Harriet Beecher Stowe, who wrote about her for *Atlantic Monthly* and wrote a new introduction to *The Narrative of Sojourner Truth.* During the Civil War Sojourner Truth raised food and clothing contributions for black regiments, and met Abraham Lincoln at the White House in 1864 where she appealed to him to end segregation on street cars.

After the Civil War she spoke widely, mainly to white audiences, and mostly on religion, "Negro" and women's rights, and on temperance, though immediately after the war she tried to organize efforts to provide jobs for black refugees.

138

"If the first woman God ever made was strong enough to turn the world upside down all alone, these women together ought to be able to turn it back, and get it right side up again! And now they is asking to do it, the men better let them."

"Religion without humanity is poor human stuff."

Gregor Mendel (1822-1884)

Born to peasant parents in what is now the Czech Republic, Mendel is the father of modern genetics. He began his research on the pea plant in the garden of the Augustinian Abbey of St. Thomas in which he was a monk. Ordained to the priesthood in 1847, Mendel was elected Abbot of his Monastery in 1868.

St. Thomas was a vibrant center of science and culture. Its friars taught and researched in philosophy, mathematics, mineralogy, and botany. The library housed many scientific works. And a mineralogical collection, botanical garden, and herbarium provided ideal labs for Mendel's lifelong research, which included not only his famous experiments on garden peas but also work in bee-culture, astronomy, and geology.

Between 1856 and 1863 Mendel cultivated and tested some 28,000 pea plants. His experiments brought forth two generalizations which later became known as Mendel's Laws of Inheritance. He observed how traits were passed down through generations. In crossbreeding pea plants to produce different combinations of traits—color, height, smoothness, and other characteristics—Mendel noted that although a given trait might not appear in every generation, the trait did not disappear. He discovered that the expression of traits hinged on whether the traits were

139

dominant or recessive, and on how these dominant and recessive traits combined.

His work remained comparatively unknown until 1900, when a new generation of botanists began finding similar results and "rediscovered" him.

Committed to God and Science, he was a creationist who rejected Darwin's evolutionary ideas, but according to Dr. Henry M. Morris, "It is remarkable that his studies clearly established the basic stability of created kinds of plants and animals, while evolutionists for many decades have labored to incorporate them somehow into the framework of Darwinism."

Louis Pasteur (1822-1895)

Pasteur may have contributed more to the saving of human lives than any other scientist. He has been called the greatest biologist of all time – the founder of microbiology. His discoveries revolutionized medicine and public health. And, he was a Christian who believed God created the diversity of life on earth.

We owe the French scientist an incalculable debt for his work in developing the "germ theory" of disease beginning in 1877, which led to the "Pasteurization" of food. He also developed vaccines for rabies, diphtheria, anthrax and many more widespread diseases.

He established the Law of Biogenesis, the principle that *only life begets life* which disproved the commonly held belief since the time of the Greeks that life could spontaneously generate out of non-life.

In Pasteur's day a majority still believed that micro-organisms came from non-living matter; for one thing, they seemed to proliferate rapidly even in distilled liquid; for another, there were so many varieties, they seemed almost chaotic and impossible to classify. Lastly, micro-organisms seemed very simple.

John Hudson Tiner, in *The History of Medicine*, said, "Pasteur rejected the theory of evolution for scientific reasons. He was the first European scientist to do so. He also rejected it on religious grounds."

Pasteur stated, "Something deep in our soul tells us that the universe is more than an arrangement of certain compounds in a mechanical equilibrium, arisen from the chaos of elements by a gradual action of Nature's forces."

Regarding germs, even in the 19th Century the mindset of doctors who, through most of history, attributed infectious disease to bad air, bad bodily fluids, comets and mystical forces had little evidence of germs. Most microscopes of that day could not detect transmissible agents so small. Pasteur, however, was convinced that the microbes he studied were the agents of infection, and proved it with a series of remarkable, life-saving discoveries.

"The more I study nature, the more I stand amazed at the work of the Creator."

William Thomson (Lord) Kelvin (1824-1907)

Kelvin was foremost among the small group of British scientists who helped to lay the foundations of modern physics. Born in Belfast, Ireland, educated at Cambridge and the University of Paris, he was Professor of Natural Sciences at Glasgow, Scotland for fifty years. Two great laws of thermodynamics are based on Lord Kelvin's conclusions: the law of equivalence and the law of transformation.

His work in applied science formed the basis for wireless and submarine telegraphy. He developed an improved mariner's compass, new sounding apparatus,

141

a tide gauge and a mirror galvanometer. His published papers on the mathematical theory of magnetism led to the theory of elasticity and better understanding of atoms and matter.

"Mathematics and dynamics fail us when we contemplate the Earth, fitted for life but lifeless, and try to imagine the commencement of life upon it. This certainly did not take place by any action of chemistry, or electricity, or crystalline grouping of molecules under the influence of force, or by any possible kind of fortuitous concourse of atoms. We must pause, face to face with the mystery and miracle of creation of living creatures."

"I cannot admit that, with regard to the origin of life, science neither affirms nor denies Creative Power. Science positively affirms Creative Power. It is not in dead matter that we live and move and have our being, but in the creating and directing Power which science compels us to accept as an article of belief."

"Overwhelming strong proofs of intelligent and benevolent design lie around us."

"If you think strongly enough you will be forced by science to the belief in God, which is the foundation of all religion. You will find science not antagonistic but helpful to religion."

Leo Tolstoy (1828-1910)

Born into a life of nobility and privilege during Czarist Russia, but so convinced of the literal truth of Jesus' command to give all you have to the poor and "come follow me," at the end of his life and to his family's consternation, Tolstoy began to give away his considerable wealth to his disciples and the peasants who ran his estate.

142

His youth and early adulthood were plagued with debauchery, violence and gambling, in fact, in his own words, "every crime imaginable." He later wrote in his book *Confession*, after great soul-searching, "I cannot recall those years without horror, loathing, and heart-rending pain." His peasants taught him a simple truth: one must live for God and not for one's self.

Best known at the author of the monumental novels *War and Peace* and *Anna Karenina*, Tolstoy's radical approach to Christianity after 1878 resulted in his expulsion from the Russian Orthodox Church. He espoused non-resistance to evil and put great emphasis on fair treatment of the poor and working class. He counseled people to look not to the State for morality but to turn within to find God. His final work, *The Kingdom of God is Within You*, is the book that won over Gandhi to the idea of non-resistance to evil.

"Don't seek God in temples. He is close to you. He is within you. Only you should surrender to Him and you will rise above happiness and unhappiness."

"Take thought, oh, men, and have faith in the Gospel, in whose teaching is your happiness. If you do not take thought, you will perish."

"The sole meaning of life is to serve humanity by contributing to the establishment of the kingdom of God, which can only be done by the recognition and profession of the truth by every man."

Max Planck (1858-1947)

German scientist Planck made many contributions to physics, but is best known as the father of quantum theory, which revolutionized our understanding of the atomic and sub-atomic world. He was awarded the Nobel Prize in Physics in 1918, "in recognition of the services he rendered to the advancement of Physics by his discovery of energy quanta."

Planck was a churchwarden from 1920 until his death, and believed in an almighty, all-knowing, beneficent God. Both science and religion wage a "tireless battle against skepticism and dogmatism, against unbelief and superstition" with the goal "toward God!"

In his 1937 lecture "Religion and Naturwissenschaft," Planck expressed the view that God is everywhere present, and held, "Since God reigns equally over all countries of the world, the whole world with all its treasures and horrors is subdued to him."

"All matter originates and exists only by virtue of a force... We must assume behind this force the existence of a conscious and intelligent Mind. This Mind is the matrix of all matter."

Planck opposed the policies of the Nazi government in Germany, particularly the persecution of Jews. However, he felt a patriotic duty to remain there rather than emigrate like so many other intellectuals and scientists. One of his two sons was brutally executed by the Gestapo for taking part in the July 1944 attempt to assassinate Adolf Hitler.

"No matter where and how far we look, nowhere do we find contradiction between religion and science"; there is "complete concordance."

George Washington Carver (1860-1943)

One of the greatest 20th Century scientists was born the child of slaves in Diamond, Missouri, during the dark days of the American Civil War. After his father was trampled to death by a team of oxen in an accident, Carver, his sister and his mother were stolen

144

by Confederate night riders. Only the infant Carver was recovered, ransomed for a horse by his parents' owner, Moses Carver, a German immigrant.

As a boy he walked eight miles to Neosho to the Lincoln School for Negro Children and eventually graduated from a Kansas high school. He would find a barn to sleep in at night, and do any odd jobs a neighbor might need, from washing dishes and cooking to planting, to pay for food and tuition.

He was accepted into Highland University in Kansas, but when he arrived to begin his studies was turned away. The school president said: "Young man, I'm afraid there has been a mistake. You failed to inform us you were colored. We do not take colored students here at Highland."

Carver was eventually accepted into the Iowa State College of Agriculture, from which he graduated in 1894 – the first African-American to do so -- and was offered a position at the college as assistant botanist specializing in hybridizing fruits.

Booker T. Washington, a friend of Abraham Lincoln, had founded Tuskegee Institute in Alabama as a place to provide blacks an opportunity for higher education. In 1896 he made Carver an unusual offer:

"I cannot offer you money, position, or fame. The first two you have. The last, from the place you now occupy, you will no doubt achieve. These things I now ask you to give up. I offer you in their place – work – hard, hard work – the challenge of bringing people from degradation, poverty and waste to full manhood."

Carver accepted the position in Alabama, a post he would hold for over 40 years. In 1897 the U.S. Department of Agriculture and the Smithsonian Institution asked Carver to catalogue medicinal flora – a collaboration which opened doors to his later advising the government on developing wartime food

145

shortage substitutes, such as the sweet potato and the peanut.

As he often told the story, he once walked out to the countryside to pray, as was his daily practice, and asked God why He made the universe. The Lord replied that was a mighty big question for a puny man. Carver tried a smaller question: why did you make man? As God kept narrowing the scope of his inquiry, he finally tried, "Mr. Creator, why did you make the peanut?"

With that, the Lord was satisfied, and told him to go into his lab and find out. In a rush of discovery Carver separated peanuts into their shells, skins, oils and meats and found all kinds of amazing properties and possibilities.

In his Tuskegee lab, Carver created not just peanut butter and peanut brittle, but soap, cooking oil, milk, rubber, glue, insecticide, malaria medicine, flour, salve, paint, cosmetics, paper, fertilizer, paving material – in all, 300 different products from the humble peanut.

"Without my Savior, I am nothing."

Sun Yat-sen (1866-1925)

The first president of modern China when the Qing Dynasty was overthrown and the Republic founded in 1912, Sun was born into a peasant family in Guangdong province in southern China just 25 km north of Macao. At age 12 he went to Hawaii to live with his elder brother where he attended an English school and then Oahu College.

When he returned home in 1883, he was greatly troubled by what he saw as a backward China controlled by warlords and corrupt officials who demanded exorbitant taxes and levies from its people.

146

In 1884 Sun transferred to the Central School of Hong Kong, later renamed Queen's College. He earned his medical license in 1892 from the Hong Kong College of Medicine for Chinese of which he was one of the first two graduates.

He was later baptized in Hong Kong by an American missionary of the Congregational Church. Sun pictured a revolution as similar to the salvation mission of the Christian church -- to transform people who would then build a just society.

Sun cautioned the growing Christian church in China to never become an instrument of foreign imperialists. He encouraged constructive debates to promote an understanding of the Gospel. He openly declared he and his family were Christians.

In 1911 the Wuchang Uprising ended almost 3000 years of imperial rule in China-- with two-thirds of the provinces declaring independence. When Sun Yat-sen was elected Provisional President of the new Republic, he quickly sought to implement democracy and reforms. But before his vision for China was fully realized, he died of liver cancer at age 58.

Sun Yat-sen once said, "Even when I die I want people to know that I am a Christian." In his will he instructed his followers "As a Christian I have wrestled with the devil for forty years. You should do likewise and believe in God."

Wernher von Braun (1912-1977)

As the father of the modern space age, his name is synonymous with rocket science: Explorer, Mariner, Voyager, Skylab, the floating space station, the Apollo missions -- America's epic voyages into the solar system and the realm of science fiction.

147

Von Braun was born in what is now Poland. Upon his Lutheran confirmation, his mother gave him his first telescope. While still in college in Berlin he received a letter from Albert Einstein in answer to his questions, and as a student, he received a grant to experiment on liquid fueled rockets. In 1934 he graduated with a PhD in physics. Always fascinated with flight of any kind, he learned to fly gliders, and in 1933, received his pilot's license for motorized aircraft.

The only rocketry work in 1930s Germany was with the military, so von Braun began his pioneering experiments at a secret site at Peenemünde, in northern Germany, where in collaboration with the Luftwaffe he began to develop liquid-fuel rocket engines for aircraft and jet-assisted takeoffs. Because of his work, he was forced to join the Nazi party.

Near the end of WW II, in February 1944, the Nazis visited von Braun's research laboratories to speed up production of the A-4, which von Braun envisioned for space exploration, but which the military renamed the V-2 for "vengeance weapon #2." When he rebuffed Heinrich Himmler's pressure to prepare rockets to attack civilian populations, von Braun was arrested in the middle of the night and charged with resisting the military use of his rockets.

Von Braun and a group of his colleagues escaped the Nazis who planned to murder the scientists rather than have them divulge technology to the Allies, but von Braun surrendered to the advancing American army in the spring of 1945, then entered the United States in September through "Operation Paperclip." He became a naturalized U.S. citizen in 1955 and worked on the ICBM program before joining NASA, where he served as Director during America's halcyon space years.

148

Perhaps his greatest achievement, the 1969 lunar landing of Apollo 11, is marked by the ***von Braun crater*** on the moon, aptly named in recognition of von Braun's contribution to space technology.

Always a Christian, he became more public in his beliefs as he aged. In his biography, *Crusader for Space*, by Frederick Ordway and Ernst Stuhlinger, Von Braun said, "Finite man cannot begin to comprehend an omnipresent, omniscient, omnipotent, and infinite God ... I find it best to accept God through faith, as an intelligent will, perfect in goodness and wisdom, revealing Himself through His creation ..."

He often stressed that "science and religion are not antagonists. On the contrary, they are sisters."

In 1972 he used his influence as a scientist to argue in a letter to the California School Board which was considering a controversial bill on the teaching of evolution that students needed to hear the case for creation:

"To be forced to believe only one conclusion—that everything in the universe happened by chance-would violate the very objectivity of science itself. Certainly there are those who argue that the universe evolved out of a random process, but what random process could produce the brain of a man or the system of the human eye?

"Some people say that science has been unable to prove the existence of a Designer... They challenge science to prove the existence of God. But, must we really light a candle to see the sun?"

Aleksandr Solzhenitsyn (1918-2008)

An Orthodox Christian and one of the 20th Century's commanding literary figures, the Russian novelist, dramatist and historian was responsible for revealing the

149

moral deprivation of the Soviet Gulag system. Awarded the Nobel Prize in Literature in 1970, he was exiled from the Soviet Union in 1974 and made his home in the United States.

Solzhenitsyn studied mathematics at Rostov State University, while at the same time taking correspondence courses from the Moscow Institute of Philosophy, Literature, and History. During World War II, he served as a commander in the Soviet Army, was involved in major action at the front, and was twice decorated. But in February 1945 while serving in East Prussia he was arrested for criticizing Joseph Stalin in private correspondence with a friend and sentenced to an eight-year term in a labor camp, followed by permanent internal exile.

Because of his ordeal, Solzhenitsyn went from avowed Communist to Gulag prisoner to outspoken advocate for the destruction of the Soviet empire. His novels – *Cancer Ward*, *The First Circle*, *Gulag Archipelago and One Day in the Life of Ivan Denisovich* -- exploded the myth of the Communist ideology and set the stage for the 1991 collapse of the Soviet Union. He has written about his own spiritual odyssey for truth in his poetry and elsewhere:

"God of the Universe! I believe again! Though I renounced You, You were with me!"

"From the heights of earthly fame I look back in wonder at the way without hope that brought me here; In this way even I have been able to spread the glow of your glory far among men!"

In his Noble Prize lecture he said of man: "it was not he who made this world, not he who gave it its meaning and directions." And he saw himself as a "tributary of a power that is greater than he, as a humble apprentice under God's heaven."

When he received the prestigious Templeton Prize in 1983, he spoke about modern moral decay, "Men have forgotten God, that's why all this has happened ... we can only reach with determination for the warm hand of God which we have so rashly and self-confidently pushed away... there is nothing else to cling to in the landslide."

Two of the 20th Century's brightest luminaries – Albert Einstein and Stephen Hawking, though not Christians -- both raised significant questions about the limits of science to explain issues that cross from the realms of naturalistic knowledge into spiritual truth. To study these men's work is to see two great intellects wrestling with ultimate reality.

Albert Einstein (1879-1955)

Einstein is probably the best known and most highly revered scientist of the twentieth century, and is associated with major revolutions in our thinking about time, gravity, and the conversion of matter to energy ($E=mc2$). Although never coming to belief in a personal God, he recognized the impossibility of a non-created universe.

The Encyclopedia Britannica says of him: "Firmly denying atheism, Einstein expressed a belief in "Spinoza's God who reveals himself in the harmony of what exists." This actually motivated his interest in science, as he once remarked to a young physicist: "I want to know how God created this world. I am not interested in this or that phenomenon, in the spectrum of this or that element. I want to know His thoughts, the rest are details."

Einstein's famous epithet on the "uncertainty principle" was "God does not play dice" - and to him this was a real statement about a God in whom he believed.

151

"My religion consists of a humble admiration of the illimitable superior spirit who reveals himself in the slight details we are able to perceive with our frail and feeble minds. That deeply emotional conviction of the presence of a superior reasoning power, which is revealed in the incomprehensible universe, forms my idea of God."

Other famous quotes of Einstein's are, "Science without religion is lame; religion without science is blind." "The more I study science the more I believe in God," and "I only trace the lines that flow from God."

Stephen Hawking (1942-   )

Considered one of the world's leading theoretical physicists, Hawking's principal fields of research are theoretical cosmology and quantum gravity. He is the Lucasian Professor of mathematics at the University of Cambridge, a post once held by Sir Isaac Newton.

Hawking has struggled most of his adult life with a motor neurological disease that has left him confined to a specially-designed wheelchair as a quadriplegic. The disease makes it necessary for him to carry out the long and complex calculations that his work requires in his head.

Though not an avowed believer, Hawking has indicated in his writings and lectures the possibility of a Creator-God as one explanation for the complexity of the universe, but he also subscribes to naturalistic theories that attempt to create a logical framework for problematic issues like DNA and the development of life.

In his bestselling book, *A Brief History of Time*, Hawking has written, ""The whole history of science has been the gradual realization that events do not happen in an arbitrary manner, but that they reflect a certain underlying order, which may or may not be divinely inspired."

"It would be very difficult to explain why the universe should have begun in just this way, except as the act of a God who intended to create beings like us."

And in replying to Einstein's famous quote, he said, "Not only does God play dice, but... he sometimes throws them where they cannot be seen."

In his public lecture, "Life in the Universe," Hawking follows a theoretical timeline from the Big Bang, approximately 15 billion years ago, to the first glimmerings of life on earth, about 5 billion years ago, in his estimation, through a series of Darwinian evolutionary stages. Here are several quotes:

"The early appearance of life on Earth suggests that there's a good chance of the spontaneous generation of life, in suitable conditions." – [*that's life from non-life.*]

"We do not know how DNA molecules first appeared. The chances against a DNA molecule arising by random fluctuations are very small." – [*even chance is unlikely.*]

"Once DNA appeared, it would have been so successful, that it might have completely replaced the earlier forms. *We don't know* [our italics] what these earlier forms would have been. *One possibility* is RNA. This is like DNA, but rather simpler, and without the double helix structure. Short lengths of RNA, could reproduce themselves like DNA, and *might eventually build up* to DNA. One cannot make nucleic acids in the laboratory, from non-living material, let alone RNA. But given 500 million years, and oceans covering most of the Earth, there might be a *reasonable probability* of RNA, being made *by chance.*"

In 1963 at the onset of his illness, at age 21, doctors predicted he would only live two or three years, but with around-the-clock care he has survived for over 40 more years.

Cassie Bernall (1981-1999)

Why include a 17-year old Colorado high school student among a pantheon of great statesmen, intellectuals, scientists and artists?

Why? Because Cassie Bernall was one of 12 students who was killed at Columbine High School April 20, 1999. Because Cassie's famous last word at gunpoint echoed around the globe, and her simple act of faith and bravery sparked a teenage spiritual revival.

She was with 40 students in the school library when the murderous rampage of two other students began. One of the gunmen reportedly asked her if she was a Christian, according to eyewitness accounts. When she said yes, she was shot at point-blank range. Later reports from others present attributed the quote to another wounded student, Valeen Schnurr – but the fact remains: Cassie was murdered in cold blood.

Those near her had heard Cassie praying aloud during the ordeal.

Cassie's mother, Misty Bernall, wrote a book about her daughter *entitled She Said Yes: The Unlikely Martyrdom of Cassie Bernall* that has been translated into Dutch, German, Italian, Korean, Swedish, Danish, Norwegian, Slovak, Romanian and Spanish.

The book recounts various tough-love steps the Bernall's took to rescue their daughter from drugs, alcohol use, witchcraft and wayward peers in Littleton, a Denver suburb. The Bernall's actions helped Cassie find faith in Jesus Christ as her Lord and Savior during a youth retreat sponsored by Littleton's West Bowles Community Church.

Rachel Scott was another Columbine student who died as a witness for her faith.

Voice of the Martyrs, an organization that tracks worldwide persecution of Christians, estimates *70 million Christians* have been murdered for their faith throughout history.

James and Marti Hefley, in their book *By Their Blood,* state more people were martyred for their faith in Jesus Christ in the 20th century than in all the previous nineteen centuries combined. Since the year 2000, approximately *165,000 are murdered each year*, according to a Regent University study. Most of those killed live in Latin America, Asia and sub-Saharan Africa.

The United Nations Commission on Human Rights on April 8, 2002 reported: "We estimate that there are more than 200 million Christians in the world today who do not have full human rights as defined by the UN Declaration of Human Rights, simply because they are Christians."

John Candelin, director of the WEA Religious Liberty Commission concluded, "We believe that this is the largest group in the world without full human rights because of their beliefs."

Why would someone be willing to die for what he or she believes? Is dying for Jesus Christ the ultimate proof of faith?

In 1956 five American missionaries killed along the Curaray River by Waodani Indians in the eastern rainforest of Ecuador were depicted in a 2006 film, *The End of the Spear.* The incident brings profound cultural changes to one of the most violent people in the world. Anthropologists document how the tribe's cultural values of murder and revenge are transformed by forgiveness and love. *Through Gates of Splendor*, by Elizabeth Elliot, tells how her husband Jim's death inspired her, her daughter and another of the missionaries' wives to bring the Gospel of Christ's love to the very people she should have hated.

A list of other Christians who had a significant impact upon the world would include prominent people in every field. Among them would be:

Augustine of Hippo (354-430), theologian, *Confessions*

Hildegard of Bingen (1098-1179), author:

"I am a feather on the breath of God."

Francis of Assisi (1182-1226), mystic:

"All creatures of our God and King/ Lift up your voice and with us sing"

Thomas Aquinas (1226-1274), theologian, *Summa Theologica:*

"In order that men might have knowledge of God, free of doubt and uncertainty, it was necessary for divine truth to be delivered to them by way of faith, being told to them as it were by God himself, who cannot lie."

Geoffrey Chaucer (1343-1400), author *The Canterbury Tales*

Fra Angelico (1395-1455), Italian artist and Dominican friar

Joan of Arc (1412-1431), French mystic, burned at the stake: "Act, and God will act."

Piero della Francesca (1420-1492), Italian artist and mathematician

Sandro Botticelli (1445-1510), Italian painter

Leonardo da Vinci (1452-1519) quintessential Renaissance man:

"I have offended God and mankind because my work didn't reach the quality it should have."

Albrecht Durer (1471-1528), German artist and writer

Titian (Tiziano Vecelli) (1488-1576), Venetian artist

Benvenuto Cellini (1500-1571) Renaissance Italian goldsmith, painter, sculptor, author:

"All works of nature created by God in heaven and on earth are works of sculpture."

John Donne (1572-1631), poet:

"As he that fears God fears nothing else, so, he that see God sees everything else."

George Herbert (1593-1633), poet:

"Prayer should be the key of the day and the lock of the night."

Rembrandt Van Rijn (1606-1669), artist:

"Painting is the grandchild of nature. It is related to God."

John Milton (1608-1674), author *Paradise Lost*

Anne Bradstreet (1612-1672), America's first poet

Daniel Defoe (1660-1731), author *Robinson Crusoe*

Jonathan Swift (1667-1745), Anglican cleric, author *Gulliver's Travels*

Alexander Pope (1688-1744), poet:

"All are but parts of one stupendous whole, Whose body Nature is, and God the soul."

Benjamin Franklin (1706-1790), statesman, inventor:

"I never doubted the existence of the Deity; that he made the world, and governed it by his Providence; that the most acceptable service of God was the doing good to man; that our souls are immortal; and that all crime will be punished, and virtue rewarded, either here or hereafter."

Carolus Linnaeus (1707-1778), Swedish botanist

Samuel Johnson (1709-1784), author:

"Trust in God is to be obtained only by repentance, obedience, and supplication, not by nourishing in our hearts a confused idea of the goodness of God, or a firm persuasion that we are in a state of grace."

Jean Jacques Rousseau (1712-1778), Swiss-French philosopher:

'Shall we say that the gospel story is the work of the imagination? My friend, such things are not imagined; and the doings of Socrates, which no one doubts, are less well attested than those of Jesus Christ.'

William Blake (1757-1827), English poet, painter, printmaker:

"The glory of Christianity is to conquer by forgiveness."

William Wordsworth (1770-1850) English Romantic poet:

"Our birth is but a sleep and a forgetting: / The soul that rises with us, our life's star, / Hath had elsewhere its setting, / And cometh from afar. / Not in entire forgetfulness, /And not in utter nakedness, / But trailing clouds of glory, do we come / From God, who is our home:" -- *Intimations of Immortality*

Samuel Taylor Coleridge (1772-1834) English Romantic poet:

"Earth with her thousand voices praises God." -- *Hymn in the Vale of Chamouni*

Chief Seattle (1790-1866), American Indian:

When he became a Christian, he instituted in his tribe a practice of communal prayers morning and evening, a practice continued after his death.

Samuel Morse (1791-1872), telegraph inventor:

"The nearer I approach the end of my pilgrimage, the clearer is the evidence of the divine origin of the Bible, the grandeur and sublimity of God's remedy for fallen man are more appreciated, and the future is illumined with hope and joy."

Gioacchino Antonio Rossini (1792-1868), composer

Franz Schubert (1797-1828), composer:

"We have trampled under our profane feet the most perfect creation of the great God."

Alexis de Tocqueville (1805-1859), French historian

Felix Mendelssohn (1809-1847), composer

Abraham Lincoln (1809-1865), 16th U.S. President:

"It is the duty of nations as well as of men to own their dependence upon the overruling power of God, and to confess their sins and transgressions in humble sorrow, yet with assured hope that genuine repentance will lead to mercy and pardon, and to recognize the sublime truth, announced in Holy Scripture, and proven by all history, that those nations only are blessed whose God is the Lord." (March 30, 1863)

Harriet Beecher Stowe (1811-1896), author *Uncle Tom's Cabin:*

"In all ranks of life the human heart yearns for the beautiful; and the beautiful things that God makes are his gift to all alike."

Franz Liszt (1811-1886), composer:

"[Music is] to ennoble, to comfort, to purify man, to bless and praise God."

Charles Dickens (1812-1870), author:

"The New Testament is the best Book the World has ever known or will know."

Soren Kierkegaard (1813-1855), philosopher:

"Father in Heaven, when the thought of Thee wakes in our hearts, let it not awaken like a frightened bird that flies about in dismay, but like a child waking from its sleep with a heavenly smile."

David Livingstone (1813-1873), African missionary-explorer:

"All that I am I owe to Jesus Christ, revealed to me in His divine Book."

Richard Wagner (1813-1883), composer:

"We await the fulfillment of Christ's pure teaching. . . the son of the Galilean carpenter, who preached the reign of universal human love."

Giuseppe Verdi (1813-1901), composer

Florence Nightingale (1820-1910), nursing pioneer:

"Today I am thirty--the age Christ began his mission. Now no more childish things. No more love. No more marriage. Now Lord let me think only of Thy Will, what Thou willest me to do. Oh Lord Thy Will, Thy Will."

Harriet Tubman (1820-1913), African-American "Moses" of anti-slavery:

"I did not work for my own benefit, but for those of my race who needed help. I know God will raise up others to take care of the future."

Fyodor Dostoyevsky (1821-1881), author *Crime and Punishment:*

"The most pressing question on the problem of faith is whether a man as a civilized being... can believe in the divinity of the Son of God, Jesus Christ, for therein rests the whole of our faith."

Antonin Dvorak (1841-1904), composer:

"I study with the birds, flowers, God and myself."

Robert Louis Stevenson (1850-1894), author, *Treasure Island*

Viscount Charles de Foucauld (1858-1916), hermit, martyr:

"As soon as I believed there was a God, I understood I could do nothing else but live for him."

Black Elk (1863-1950), holy man of the Ogalala Lakota (Sioux):

He converted to Christianity in 1904 and led a very active life as a Catholic catechist and Christian missionary to his fellow Native Americans until his death.

"Since the last Sioux Congress and at the present time (1906), I have visited the Rosebud Reservation. The people there told me that they want churches built on their own districts. I was pleased to hear these people are interested in God.

"I spoke mainly on Jesus-- when he was on earth, the teachings and his sufferings. I myself do a lot of these things. I suffer and I try to teach my people the things that I wanted them to learn, but it's never done."

G.K. Chesterton (1874-1936), writer:

"One of the chief uses of religion is that it makes us remember our coming from darkness, the simple fact that we are created."

Charles Ives (1874-1954), composer

Igor Stravinsky (1882-1971), composer:

"The more one separates oneself from the canons of the Christian church, the further one distances oneself from the truth."

Gerard Manley Hopkins (1844-1889), priest, poet:

"The world is charged with the grandeur of God."

Wilbur (1867 - 1912) and **Orville Wright** (1871 - 1948), aviators: First controlled, powered, air flight on December 17, 1903.

T. S. Eliot (1888-1965), author *The Waste Land*

Boris Pasternak (1890-1960), Nobel prize winning author of *Dr. Zhivago*:

"You ask, who orders? / --Omnipotent God of details, / Omnipotent God of love."

Charles de Gaulle (1890-1970), French president

J.R.R. Tolkien (1892-1973), author, *The Lord of the Rings*

Pearl S. Buck (1892-1973), Nobel Prize winning author:

"A dog barks when his master is attacked. I would be a coward if I saw that God's truth is attacked and yet would remain silent."

C. S. Lewis (1898-1963), author *The Narnia Chronicles*

Dag Hammarskjöld (1905-1961), Swedish General Secretary of the United Nations:

"God does not die on the day when we cease to believe in a personal deity, but we die on the day when our lives cease to be illumined by the steady radiance, renewed daily, of a wonder, the source of which is beyond all reason."

Dietrich Bonhoeffer (1906-1945), theologian and Nazi resister:

"It is not the religious act that makes the Christian, but participation in the sufferings of God in the secular life."

Charles Hard Townes (1915-   ), 1964 Nobel Prize in Physics, laser inventor:

"The more we know about the cosmos and evolutionary biology, the more they seem inexplicable without some aspect of design. And for me that inspires faith."

Flannery O'Connor (1925-1964), author:

"When a book leaves your hands, it belongs to God. He may use it to save a few souls or to try a few others, but I think that for the writer to worry is to take over God's business."

César Chávez (1931-1933**),** labor leader, founder United Farm Workers:

"We are certain God's will is that all men share in the good things this earth produces."

Svetlana Alliluyeva (1928-2011), daughter of Soviet dictator Josef Stalin

Seamus Heaney (1939-2013), Irish Nobel prize winning poet:

"God is a foreman with certain definite views / Who orders life in shifts of work and leisure."

Garrison Keillor (1942-   ), American humorist, author:

"Thank you, God, for this good life and forgive us if we do not love it enough."

Lech Wałęsa (1943-   ), Polish human rights activist and founder of *Solidarity*

Francis Collins (1950-   ), Director, National Human Genome Research Institute:

He has also written on religious matters in articles and in *Faith and the Human Genome* he states the importance to him of "the literal and historical Resurrection of Jesus Christ from the dead, which is the cornerstone of what I believe."

Melinda Gates (1961-   ), philanthropist:

Bill and Melinda Gates Foundation, dedicated to improving health and education, especially in poor nations, made $1.4 billion in grant payments in 2005 compared to the United Nations Educational, Scientific and Cultural Organization, or UNESCO's budget of $610 million. She often quotes the words of Jesus: "*To whom much is given, much will be required.*"

Reasonable Conclusion #10 – Throughout history the greatest scientists, writers, artists, musicians and statesmen have honored and followed Jesus Christ. What about you?

166

In A Nutshell

[14] After John was put in prison, Jesus went into Galilee, proclaiming the good news of God. [15] "The time has come," he said. "The kingdom of God has come near. *Repent and believe the good news*!"

[16] As Jesus walked beside the Sea of Galilee, he saw Simon and his brother Andrew casting a net into the lake, for they were fishermen. [17] *"Come, follow me,"* Jesus said, "and I will send you out to fish for people." [18] At once they left their nets and followed him.

Mark 1:14-20

Made in the USA
Monee, IL
09 November 2020

47116259R00100